CREDO PERSPECTIVES

VOLUMES ALREADY PUBLISHED

CREDO PERSPECTIVES

PLANNED AND EDITED BY

RUTH NANDA ANSHEN

A BELIEVING HUMANISM:

My Testament, 1902-1965

BY

MARTIN BUBER

Translated and with an Introduction
and Explanatory Comments by
MAURICE FRIEDMAN

SIMON AND SCHUSTER
NEW YORK

CONTENTS

7

CREDO PERSPECTIVES

Their Meaning and Function

Credo Perspectives suggest that twentieth-century man is living in one of the world's most challenging periods, unprecedented in history, a dynamic period when he has almost unlimited choices for good and evil. In all civilizations of the world of our modern epoch, in both socialistic and capitalistic societies, we are faced with the compelling need to understand more clearly the forces that dominate our world and to modify our attitudes and behavior accordingly. And this will only happen if our best minds are persuaded and assembled to concentrate on the nature of this new epoch in evolutionary and moral history. For we are confronted with a very basic change. Man has intervened in the evolutionary process and he must better appreciate this fact with its influence on his life and work, and then try to develop the wisdom to direct the process, to recognize the mutable and the immutable elements in his moral nature and the relationship between freedom and order.

The authors in this series declare that science now permits us to say that "objective" nature, the world which alone is "real" to us as the one in which we all, scientists included, are born, love, hate, work, reproduce and die, is the world given us by our senses and our minds—a world in which the sun crosses the sky from east to west, a world of three-dimensional space, a world of values which we, and we alone, must make. It is true that scientific knowledge about macroscopic or subatomic events may enable us to perform many acts we were unable to per-

form before. But it is as inhabitants of this human world
that we perform them and must finally recognize that there
is a certain kind of scientific "objectivity" that can lead us
to know everything but to understand nothing.

The symbol of *Credo Perspectives* is the Eye of Osiris.
It is the inner eye. Man sees in two ways: with his physical
eyes, in an empirical sensing or *seeing* by direct observation, and also by an indirect envisaging. He possesses in
addition to his two sensing eyes a single, image-making,
spiritual and intellectual Eye. And it is the *in-sight* of this
inner Eye that purifies and makes sacred our understanding
of the nature of things; for that which was shut fast has
been opened by the command of the inner Eye. And we
become aware that to believe is to see.

This series is designed to present a kind of intellectual
autobiography of each author, to portray the nature and
meaning of his creative process and to show the relevance
of his work to his feelings and aspirations. In it we hope
also to reflect the influence of the work on the man and
on society, and to point to the freedom, or lack of freedom,
to choose and pursue one profession rather than another.
For the creator in any realm must surrender himself to a
passionate pursuit of his labors, guided by deep personal
intimations of an as yet undiscovered reality.

Credo Perspectives hope to unlock a consciousness that
at first sight may seem to be remote but is proved on ac-
quaintance to be surprisingly immediate, since it stems
from the need to reconcile the life of action with the life
of contemplation, of practice with principle, of thought
with feeling, of knowing with being. For the whole meaning of *self* lies within the observer, and its shadow is cast
naturally on the object observed. The divorce of man from
his work, the division of man into an eternal and temporal
half, results in an estrangement of man from his creative
source, and ultimately from his fellows and from himself.

The hope of this series is to suggest that the universe

itself is a vast entity where man will be lost if it does not converge in the person; for material forces or energies, or impersonal ideals, or scientifically objectified learning are meaningless without their relevance for human life and their power to disclose, even in the dark tendencies of man's nature, a law transcending man's arbitrariness.

For the personal is a far higher category than the abstract universal. Personality itself is an emotional, not an intellectual, experience; and the greatest achievement of knowledge is to combine the personal within a larger unity, just as in the higher stages of development the parts that make up the whole acquire greater and greater independence and individuality within the context of the whole. Reality itself is the harmony which gives to the component particulars of a thing the equilibrium of the whole. And while physical observations are ordered with direct reference to the experimental conditions, we have in sensate experience to do with separate observations whose correlation can only be indicated by their belonging to the wholeness of mind.

It is the endeavor of the authors to show that man has reached a turning point in consciousness, that his relationship with his creativity demands a clarification that can widen and deepen his understanding of the nature of reality. Work is made for man, not man for work. This series hopes to demonstrate the sacramental character of work, which is more easily achieved when the principal objects of our attention have taken on a symbolic form that is generally recognized and accepted; and this suggests a *law* in the relationship of a person and his chosen discipline: that it is valuable only when the spiritual, the creative, life is strong enough to insist on some expression through symbols. For no work can be based on material, technological, historical, or physical aspirations alone.

The human race is now entering upon a new phase of evolutionary consciousness and progress, a phase in which, impelled by the forces of evolution itself, it must converge upon itself and convert itself into one single human organism infused by a reconciliation of knowing and being in their inner unity and destined to make a qualitative leap into a higher form of consciousness that would transcend and complement individual consciousness as we know it, or otherwise destroy itself. For the entire universe is one vast field, potential for incarnation and achieving incandescence here and there of reason and spirit. And in the whole world of *quality* with which by the nature of our minds we necessarily make contact, we here and there apprehend pre-eminent value. This can be achieved only if we recognize that we are unable to focus our attention on the particulars of a whole without diminishing our comprehension of the whole, and of course, conversely, we can focus on the whole only by diminishing our comprehension of the particulars which constitute the whole.

The kind of knowledge afforded by mathematical physics ever since the seventeenth century has come more and more to furnish mankind with an ideal for all knowledge. This error about the nature of knowledge it is the hope of this series to expose. For knowledge is a process, not a product and the results of scientific investigation do not carry with them self-evident implications. There are now, however, signs of new centers of resistance among men everywhere in almost all realms of knowledge. Many share the conviction that a deep-seated moral and philosophical reform is needed concerning our understanding of the nature of man and the nature of knowledge in relation to the work man is performing, in relation to his *credo* and his life.

Credo Perspectives constitute an endeavor to alter the prevailing conceptions, not only of the nature of knowledge and work, but also of creative achievements in general, as well as of the human agent who inquires and creates, and of the entire fabric of the culture formed by such activities. In other words, this is an endeavor to show that what we see and what we do are no more and no less than what we are.

It is the endeavor of *Credo Perspectives* to define the new reality in which the estrangement of man from his work, resulting in the self-estrangement in man's existence, is overcome. This new reality is born through the reconciliation of what a man *knows* with what a man *is*. Being itself in all its presuppositions and implications can only be understood through the totality, through wholeness. St. Paul, who, like Isaiah before him, went into the marketplace not to secularize truth but to proclaim it, taught man that the "new creation" could be explained only by conquering the daemonic cleavages, the destructive split, in soul and cosmos. And that fragmentation always destroys a unity, produces a tearing away from the source and thereby creates disunity and isolation. The fruit can never be separated from the tree. The Tree of Life can never be disjoined from the Tree of Knowledge for both have *one and the same* root. And if man allows himself to fall into isolation, if he seeks to maintain a self segregated from the totality of which he is a necessary part, if he chooses to be unrelated to the original context of all created things in which he too has his place—including his own labors— then this act of apostasy bears fruit in the demiurgical presumption of *magic,* a form of animism in which man seeks an authority of the self, placing himself above the law of the universe by attempting to separate the inseparable. He thus creates an unreal world after having destroyed or deserted the real. And in this way the method of analysis, of scientific objectivity, which is good and necessary in its right place, is endowed with a destructive power when it is allowed to usurp a place for which it is not fitted.

The naturalist principle that man is the measure of all things has been shattered more than ever in our own age by the question, "What is the measure of man?" Post-

modern man is more profoundly perplexed about the nature of man than his ancestors were. He is on the verge of
spiritual and moral insanity. He does not know who he is.
And having lost the sense of who and what he is, he fails
to grasp the meaning of his fellow man, of his vocation
and of the nature and purpose of knowledge itself. For
what is not understood cannot be known. And it is this
cognitive faculty which is frequently abrogated by the
"scientific" theory of knowledge, a theory that refuses to
recognize the existence of comprehensive entities as dis-
tinct from their particulars. The central act of knowing is
indeed that form of comprehension which is never absent
from any process of knowing and is finally its ultimate
sanction.

Science itself acknowledges as real a host of entities that
cannot be described completely in materialistic or mecha-
nistic terms, and it is this transcendence out of the domain
of science into a region from which science itself can be
appraised that *Credo Perspectives* hope to define. For the
essence of the ebb and flow of experience, of sensations,
the richness of the immediacy of directly apprehended
knowledge, the metaphysical substance of what assails our
being, is the very act itself of sensation and affection and
therefore must escape the net of rational analysis, yet is
intimately related to every cognitive act. It is this increas-
ing intellectual climate that is calling into birth once more
the compelling Socratic questions, "What is the purpose
of life, the meaning of work?" "What is man?" Plato himself could give us only an indirect answer: "Man is declared to be that creature who is constantly in search of
himself, a creature who at every moment of his existence
must examine and scrutinize the conditions of his existence.
He is a being in search of meaning."

From this it is evident that there is present in the universe a *law* applicable to all nature including man and his
work. Life itself then is seen to be a creative process

elaborating and maintaining *order* out of the randomness of matter, endlessly generating new and unexpected structures and properties by building up associations that qualitatively transcend their constituent parts. This is not to diminish the importance of "scientific objectivity." It is, however, to say that the mind possesses a quality that cannot be isolated or known exclusively in the sense of objective knowledge. For it consists in that elusive humanity in us, our self, that knows. It is that inarticulate awareness that includes and *comprehends* all we know. It consists in the irreducible active voice of man and is recognized only in other things, only when the circle of consciousness closes around its universe of events.

Our hope is to point to a new dimension of morality—not that of constraint and prohibition but a morality that lies as a fountainhead within the human soul, a morality of aspiration to spiritual experience. It suggests that necessity is laid upon us to infer entities that are not observed and are not observable. For an unseen universe is necessary to explain the seen. The flux is seen, but to account for its structure and its nature we infer particles of various kinds to serve as the vertices of the changing patterns, placing less emphasis on the isolated units and more on the structure and nature of relations. The process of knowing involves an immaterial becoming, an immaterial identification, and finally, knowledge itself is seen to be a dependent variable of immateriality. And somewhere along this spiritual pilgrimage man's pure observation is relinquished and gives way to the deeper experience of awe, for there can be no explanation of a phenomenon by searching for its origin but only by discerning its immanent law—this quality of transcendence that abides even in matter itself. The present situation in the world and the vast accretion of knowledge have produced a serious anxiety which may be overcome by re-evaluating the character, kinship, logic and operation of man in relation to his work. For work implies goals and intimately affects the person performing the work. Therefore the correlation and relatedness of ideas, facts and values that are in perpetual interplay could emerge from these volumes as they point to the inner synthesis and organic unity of man and his labors. For though no labor alone can enrich the person, no enrichment can be achieved without absorbing and intense labor. We then experience a unity of faith, labor and grace which prepares the mind for receiving a truth from sources over which it has no control. This is especially true since the great challenge of our age arises out of man's inventions in relation to his life.

Thus *Credo Perspectives* seek to encourage the perfection not only of man's works but also and above all the fulfillment of himself as a person. And so we now are summoned to consider not only man in the process of development as a human subject but also his influence on the object of his investigation and creation. Observation alone is interference. The naïve view that we can observe any system and predict its behavior without altering it by the very act of observation was an unjustified extrapolation from Newton's *Celestial Mechanics*. We can observe the moon or even a satellite and predict its behavior without perhaps appreciably interfering with it, but we cannot do this with an amoeba, far less with a man and still less with a society of men. It is the heart of the question of the nature of work itself. If we regard our labors as a process of shaping or forming, then the fruits of our labors play the part of a mold by which we ourselves are shaped. And this means, in the preservation of the identity of the knower and the known, that cognition and generation, that is, creation, though in different spheres, are nevertheless alike.

It is hoped that the influence of such a series may help to overcome the serious separations between function and meaning and may show that the extraordinary crisis through which the world is passing can be fruitfully met by recognizing that knowledge has not been completely dehumanized and has not totally degenerated into a mere notebook overcrowded with formulas that few are able to understand or apply.

For mankind is now engaged in composing a new theme. Life never manifests itself in negative terms. And our hope lies in drawing from every category of work a conviction that nonmaterial values can be discovered in positive, affirmative, visible things. The estrangement between the temporal and nontemporal man is coming to an end, community is inviting communion, and a vision of the human condition more worthy of man is engendered, connecting ever more closely the creative mind with the currents of spiritual energy which breaks for us the bonds of habit and keeps us in touch with the permanence of being through our work.

And as, long ago, the Bearers of Bread were succeeded by the Bearers of Torches, so now, in the immediacies of life, it is the image of man and his vocation that can rekindle the high passion of humanity in its quest for light. Refusing to divorce work from life or love from knowledge, it is action, it is passion that enhances our being.

We live in an expanding universe and also in the moral infinite of that other universe, the universe of man. And along the whole stretched arc of this universe we may see that extreme limit of complicity where reality seems to shape itself within the work man has chosen for his realization. Work then becomes not only a way of knowledge, it becomes even more a way of life—of life in its totality. For the last end of every maker is himself.

"And the places that have been desolate for ages shall be built in thee: thou shalt raise up the foundations of generation and generation; and thou shalt be called the repairer of the fences, turning the paths into rest."*

RUTH NANDA ANSHEN

---

* Isaiah, 58:12.

MARTIN BUBER'S CREDO

Maurice Friedman

WHEN DR. RUTH NANDA ANSHEN approached me about a book of Martin Buber's that might be suitable for inclusion in her *Credo Perspectives,* I suggested his *Nachlese.* As the German title implies, this final volume of Buber's writings is the gleaning that comes at the end of the harvest, as in the Book of Ruth, where the poor go after the reapers to pick up the gleanings. When Buber selected them only a few months before his death, on June 13, 1965, his only principle of selection was "that and only that . . . which appears to me today as a valid expression, worthy of surviving, of an experience, a feeling, a decision, yes even of a dream." Yet Buber himself could just for this reason call this book as a whole a "testament." As such, it does, indeed, belong in the *Credo Perspectives.*

If the dictionary meaning of "credo" is "a creed; a set of professed opinions," the Latin original literally means "I believe." For Martin Buber, the "I" of "I believe" could never be some self-sufficient thinker isolated from direct and mutual relationship with a "Thou," nor could what he believed be a monological expression of a set of abstract principles. True faith to Buber, as *Two Types of Faith,** his study of Jesus and Paul, makes clear, is not "I believe that such and such is true" (*pistis*) but unconditional trust in the relationship with God (the Biblical *emunah* which Buber also saw as at the heart of Jesus' teaching). I once wrote to Buber that if I were to write my book *Martin Buber: The Life of Dialogue*†

---

* New York: Harper Torchbooks (paperback), 1961.

† New York: Harper Torchbooks, 1960.

again, I would add a concluding chapter to show existential
trust as the heart of his teaching, an insight which Buber confirmed in his reply. In my forthcoming book, on the way in
which Buber's thought grew out of the events and meetings
of his life—*Martin Buber: Encounter on the Narrow Ridge**
—I am endeavoring to show how every one of Buber's basic
distinctions—"I-Thou" and "I-It," "realizing" and "orienting," *"emunah"* and *"pistis,"* "prophetic" and "apocalyptic,"
"devotio" and *"gnosis,"* "being" and "seeming"—is rooted
in the presence or absence of basic trust.

Some of Buber's critics have stated that his faith is pure
relationship without content—a misunderstanding which is
only possible for those who have never grasped Buber's existentialism of dialogue as "grounded on the certainty that
the meaning of existence is open and accessible in the actual
lived concrete." This is not, of course, the content of absolute
objective principles, whether in the form of a theological
creed or of Platonic truths. But neither is it the mere phe-
nomenological analysis of existence offered us by many modern existentialists, still less the current emphasis upon *having*
experience. It is rather the wholly particular content of each
moment of lived dialogue in which the reality one meets is
neither subjectivized nor objectivized but *responded* to.

> That meaning is open and accessible in the actual lived con-
> crete does not mean it is to be won and possessed through any
> type of analytical or synthetic investigation or through any
> type of reflection upon the lived concrete. Meaning is to be
> experienced in living action and suffering itself, in the unre-
> duced immediacy of the moment. Of course, he who aims at
> the experiencing of experience will necessarily miss the mean-
> ing, for he destroys the spontaneity of the mystery. *Only he
> reaches the meaning who stands firm, without holding back or
> reservation, before the whole might of reality and answers it*

---

* New York: McGraw-Hill Books, 1968.

in a living way. He is ready to confirm with his life the meaning which he has attained.*

The certainty that the meaning of existence is open and accessible in the "lived concrete" is not the certainty of dogma, creed, or metaphysics, but the "holy insecurity" of the "narrow ridge" where one has no assured continuity of meaning yet at one time and another "meets the unnamed Meeter." Buber's "believing humanism" accordingly, is really the humanism of "the life of dialogue." What Buber says of Theodor Heuss is equally true of himself: his humanism is not that of a program but of "the persevering and withstanding steadiness of personal existence." Its content, like the statement of Heuss which Buber quotes, is "the 'human trust' that grows in the depths." Its form, as Buber himself says in the Erasmus Prize address from which I have taken the title, is not faith and humanity in two separate compartments, but a full interpenetration of one by the other. One can say, in truth, that Buber's humanism and his faith each find in the other their deepest ground.

Buber's believing humanism, as a result, is not a *credo quia absurdum est,* even in the modern form of Kierkegaard's "leap of faith." It is faith as witness, as faithful testimony and response in the cruel as well as the gracious situations of life. For this reason, the only appropriate form which Martin Buber's credo could take is precisely this selection— made to the stern and gentle melody of "that fiddler" who fiddled when the All had became silent and bore him away from life to the meeting with eternity. If Buber deemed these essays, sketches, talks, and poems worthy of surviving, it was not because they seemed to him adequate statements of objective truth, but because they witnessed to the only truth he

---

* Martin Buber, *Eclipse of God. Studies in the Relation between Religion and Philosophy* (New York: Harper Torchbooks, 1957), "Religion and Philosophy," trans. by Maurice Friedman, p. 35. Italics added.

knew—that human truth that arises in response to the events and meetings of our lives. It is for this reason that Buber declined to give titles to the ten sections in which the book is divided. To analyze and synthesize the nuggets of belief that are found here would be to destroy their character as witness and as truth.

These fragments come from a span of over sixty years of Buber's life—almost the whole of his long career as a writer. They reveal better than any other single volume the great breadth and profundity of his writings. The situations in which these responses arose are as varied as the Jewish renaissance movement led by Buber and his friends within early Zionism, the First World War, the promise and confusion of the nineteen twenties, the menacing shadow of Hitler and German anti-Semitism, the Second World War, and the Cold War and the age of atom bombs and space travel that followed. The subjects range from literary studies to meetings with spiritual and political figures, from statements on education, religion, philosophy, psychotherapy, art, architecture, politics, and ethics, to wholly personal expressions in poems and messages of thanks. Yet the ten divisions to which Buber refers in his foreword cannot be grasped along any of these lines.

What remains to my task is to supply such information as is essential to the English-speaking reader's understanding of what Buber responded to and of the way in which he responded. Since to place this information at the bottom of each selection would destroy the simplicity and readability of the book, I am for the most part appending it at the end of the book under the title "Explanatory Comments."

A special word is needed here about the relation between *A Believing Humanism* and Buber's earlier collection of essays *Pointing the Way*. When I edited the latter book, I included, partly at Buber's suggestion, several essays that did not appear in the German original *Hinweise* while leaving out some that had appeared elsewhere or that did not seem to me suited to the English-speaking reader. Three of the essays which I included in *Pointing the Way* and which are not in *Hinweise* were taken up by Buber for *Nachlese*. If I had been able to consult with Buber about *A Believing Humanism* as I was about the many other books of his that I edited and translated, it may well be that he would have said to omit these three essays since they are already published in English. Since this was not possible and since this book is so clearly a last will and testament of a highly personal nature, Rafael Buber (Buber's son and heir) and I both felt that the book should be left exactly as it is. Thanks to the kind permission of Harper and Row, we have been able to include in *A Believing Humanism* the essays "Healing Through Meeting," "China and Us," and "Genuine Dialogue and the Possibilities of Peace," all of which are already to be found in *Pointing the Way*. It is not without significance that two of these three essays are from the third part of *Pointing the Way,* which Dag Hammarskjøld wrote me that he wanted to translate into Swedish, and that Buber's reminiscence of the Secretary General of the United Nations appears along with them in *A Believing Humanism.* "I think that Martin Buber has made a major contribution in these essays" on politics, community, and peace, said Hammarskjøld to the press, "and I would like to make them more broadly known."

Acknowledgment must also be made to Dr. Homer A. Jacks, for permission to include in *A Believing Humanism* my translation of "A Realist of the Spirit" from the book which he edited, *To Dr. Albert Schweitzer. A Festschrift Commemorating His Eightieth Birthday* (1955). I should also like to thank Mr. Moshe Klibanoff, now of Jerusalem, Israel, for his insight into the relation between Buber's last poem "The Fiddler" and Buber's treatment of "being and seeming" and "existential guilt" in *The Knowledge of Man.*

Finally, I should like to thank my colleague, Dr. Elizabeth D. Woodworth, Associate Professor of German at Manhattanville, for her unusual generosity and devotion in going through the whole manuscript, spotting errors, helping to interpret difficult passages, and giving discerning advice as to the rendering of certain words and images in the poetry. Both Rafael Buber and I felt that the organic wholeness of *A Believing Humanism* makes it essential to include in it the few poems that Buber selected from among the many that he wrote over his lifetime. At the same time, since it is not possible to do full justice to poetry in translation, we felt that it would enhance the book for many readers to include on the facing page the German original as is done in the case of Rilke and other German poets today.

MAURICE FRIEDMAN

Manhattanville College
Purchase, New York
January 1967

AUTHOR'S FOREWORD

To the three publications in which I have assembled those of my writings that (for various reasons) seem worthy of being preserved—the book *Hinweise** [*Hints*] of 1953, the three large volumes of my works (1. *Writings on Philosophy, 2. Writings on the Bible, 3. Writings on Hasidism*)† of 1962 to 1964, and that collected volume intended to supplement them, if from a wholly other point of view, *Der Jude und sein Judentum* [*The Jew and His Jewishness*]‡ of 1963—I allow here a fourth and last to follow.

This is an after-reading, a gleaning, in the exact sense of the word. Accordingly the point of view that has here determined the selection (a selection has also taken place this time) could not be grasped as before in an objective formulation. In the selection of what has been taken from the literary yield of all these years—the oldest piece stems from 1902, the newest from 1964—no other principle has ruled than this: that and only that belongs here which appears to me today as a valid, as a survival-worthy expression of an experience, a feeling, a decision, yes even of a dream. Ac-

---

* *Gesammelte Essays.* Zurich: Mannesse Verlag. [Most, but not all of *Hinweise,* was translated in *Pointing the Way,* ed. & trans. with an Introduction by Maurice Friedman. New York: Harper Torchbooks, 1963. M.F.]

† Kösel Verlag, Munich, and Verlag Lambert Schneider, Heidelberg. [The titles of the three volumes in German are I. *Schriften zur Philosophie,* II. *Schriften zur Bibel,* III. *Schriften zum Chassidismus.* M.F.]

‡ *Gesammelte Reden und Aufsatze* [*Collected Addresses and Essays*]. Cologne: Joseph Melzer Verlag.

27

cordingly I have also included here some of my poems, unpublished and a few of them already published (I have only
rarely allowed my poems to be printed). In accordance with
this context, I could also probably call the whole a witness.

In consonance with the character of the book, the ten divisions into which it falls bear no subtitles; but one will certainly recognize without difficulty what is the dominant motif
in each one of them.

The sorting and sifting of the manifold material was made
possible for me by the fundamental and untiring help of my
secretary, Mrs. Margot Cohn, to whom at this place a special
thanks is due.

MARTIN BUBER

Jerusalem
February 9, 1965

REMINISCENCE

IN THESE DAYS, which lead me to reflect in a special manner on the course of my life, the memory of the earlier stages of my relationship to the German language is also awakened anew.

Born in Vienna, I came in my early childhood to Lvov (Lemberg), the capital city of the Galician province in which an unusual multiplicity of language stamped upon me indelibly the fact of very different peoples living next to one another. In my grandfather's as in my father's house the German language predominated, but the street and the school were Polish; only the Jewish quarter rustled with the rough and tender Yiddish, and in the synagogue there resounded, alive as ever, the great voice of Hebrew antiquity. Not merely in these, but also in the German word, there dwelt a pathos. That came about through the fact that my grandmother, Adele Buber, who reared me until my fourteenth year, guarded this language like a hidden treasure that has been discovered. Once when she was fifteen years old, she kept hidden in the storehouse the German books forbidden in her home ghetto as worldly. I still possess her copy of Jean Paul's *Levana,* the teachings of which she wanted to use in the education of her future children and later really did use. In the time of my childhood, she inscribed in the tall, narrow account books—between the accounts of income and expenditures of the great estate, the management of which she never let out of her sight—sometimes sayings of the revered minds, sometimes her own inspirations, all in a pithy and firm German. In this language atmosphere I grew up.

29

In my eighteenth year I came to the University in Vienna. What made the strongest impression on me there was the *Burgtheater* into which, often day after day, I rushed up three flights after several hours of "posting myself" in order to capture a place in the highest gallery. There, by men who were called players, the German language was spoken. I understood: in the books that I had read the signs were indicated; here first did they become the sounds that were meant. That was a great instruction. But there was also a charming seduction in it: here first was the primordial gold of speech poured into the laps of heirs who had taken no pains to earn it. "Let the heir be a squanderer," so the "Song of Life" began which once resounded to me from a pamphlet bought on the street. It was composed by someone named Hofmannsthal, someone, I soon learned, only four years older than myself. I understood: the German language was not only brought to its full spokenness in this city; it also brought into being ever new poetry. But around all this there was a wonderful ease, that of the man who lived, according to the poem, "like him whom no power threatens from behind." This nonchalance of the heir who "squandered the treasures of antiquity" enchanted my heart; it penetrated into my reading and writing.

Two decades passed before, in the storm of the World War, which made manifest the innermost threat to man, I struggled through to the strict service of the word and earned the heritage with as much difficulty as if I had never supposed that I possessed it. When several years later I saw Hofmannsthal again after a long interval, I marked in his traits, gestures, and accent what his late work had already communicated to me: that he had gone the same way of renunciation, of effort, and of new beginning. In language as in all realms of human existence no continuance can any longer be assured except through sacrifice.

TO CREATE NEW WORDS

IN THE STATEMENT that was sent to me it says that the task of the academy which is to be founded is "to create words of spiritual value for the speech of Western peoples."

As highly as I esteem the possibilities of a community of like-minded men and their working power, that seems to me to overstep in principle the functions of such a community. The generation, the creation of words is for me one of the most mysterious processes of the life of the spirit. Indeed, I confess that to my insight there is no *essential* difference between what I here call the creation of words and that which has been called the coming forward of the Logos. The coming into being of words is a mystery that is consummated in the enkindled, open soul of the world-producing, world-discovering man. Only such a word engendered in the spirit can become creative in man. Therefore, in my view it cannot be the task of a community to *make* it. Rather it seems to me that a body such as is planned by you and your friends may and should set as its goal only a *purification* of the word. What is needed is not teaching the use of new words but fighting the misuse of the great old words.

BEKENNTNIS
DES SCHRIFTSTELLERS

Für Ernst Simon

Ich bin einst mit leichtem Kiele
Ums Land der Legende geschifft,
Durch Sturm der Taten und Spiele,
Unlässig den Blick nach dem Ziele
Und im Blut das berückende Gift—
Da ist einer auf mich niedergefahren,
Der fasste mich an den Haaren
Und sprach: Nun stelle die Schrift!

Von Stund an hält die Galeere
Mir Gehirn und Hände im Gang,
Das Ruder schreibt Charaktere,
Mein Leben verschmäht seine Ehre
Und die Seele vergisst, dass sie sang.
Alle Stürme müssen stehn und sich neigen,
Wenn grausam zwingend im Schweigen
Der Spruch des Geistes erklang.

Hau in den Fels deine Taten, Welt!
In der Flut ist Schrift erstellt.

CONFESSION
OF THE AUTHOR

For Ernst Simon

Once with a light keel
I shipped out to the land of legends
Through the storm of deeds and play,
With my gaze fixed on the goal
And in my blood the beguiling poison—
Then one descended to me
Who seized me by the hair
And spoke: Now render the Scriptures!

From that hour on the galley
Keeps my brain and hands on course,
The rudder writes characters,
My life disdains its honor
And the soul forgets that it sang.
All storms must stand and bow
When cruelly compelling in the silence
The speech of the spirit resounds.

Hammer your deeds in the rock, world!
The Word is wrought in the flood.

IN HEIDELBERG

THAT THE University of Heidelberg has awarded me an honorary doctorate has a special significance for me intertwined with my life memory and my life history. I have not studied at Heidelberg, to be sure, but in the world of imagination of young men here was the great school *kat exochen,* the exemplary abode of great teaching. Shortly after the beginning of the First World War—which at that time I had already experienced as the beginning of the crisis of mankind—I found living in Berlin all too painful. When I looked around for a quieter dwelling place, my choice was influenced by the closeness to Heidelberg.

The atmospheric nearness of this organic-spiritual center was for more than two decades helpful in my life and work. In the years until the upheaval of 1918–1919 this influence took the form above all of personal contact with Max Weber; today the hours which I was privileged to spend in the house on the Neckar are still vividly present to me. From the time of the Weimar Republic, there continue to live in my memory the walks on the "philosopher's way" to which I ever again invited the philosophers and scholars who visited me in those years. But even from the last years that I spent in Germany, until the spring of 1938, years when I only rarely journeyed to Heidelberg, I have preserved a good memory: that of the visits of some young men from Heidelberg—seemingly closely connected with the ruling regime—who came to me in order to complain of their sufferings.

All this has interwoven itself for me now, stronger than

ever before, as I composed this statement that my Heidelberg friend and publisher Lambert Schneider will read aloud there. I feel the high honor that the University of Heidelberg has accorded to me as the crown of all these life connections.

ELIJAHU

Du wolltest wie ein Sturmwind niedergehen
Und wie der Föhn im Tun gewaltig sein,
Du wolltest Wesen hin zu Wesen wehen
Und Menschenseelen geisselnd benedein,
In heissem Wirbel müde Herzen mahnen
Und Starres rühren zu bewegtem Licht,
—Du suchtest mich auf deinen Sturmesbahnen
Und fandst mich nicht.

Du wolltest wie ein Feuer aufwärts drängen
Und alles tilgen, was dir nicht bestand,
Du wolltest sonnenmächtig Welten sengen
Und Welten läutern in geweihtem Brand,
Mit jäher Wucht ein junges Nichts entzünden
Zu neuen Werdens seligem Gedicht,
—Du suchtest mich in deinen Flammengründen
Und fandst mich nicht.

Da kam mein Bote über dich und legte
Dein Ohr ans stille Leben meiner Erde,
Da fühltest du, wie Keim an Keim sich regte,
Und dich umfing des Wachsens Allgebärde,
Blut schlug an Blut, und dich bezwang das Schweigen,
Das ewig volle, weich und mütterlich,
—Da musstest du dich zu dir selber neigen,
Da fandst du mich.

ELIJAH

You wanted to descend like a storm wind
And to be mighty in deed like the tempest,
You wanted to blow being to being
And bless human souls while scourging them,
To admonish weary hearts in the hot whirlpool
And to stir the rigid to agitated light,
—You sought me on your stormy paths
And did not find me.

You wanted to soar upward like a fire
And wipe out all that did not stand your test,
Sun-powerful, you wanted to scorch worlds
And to refine worlds in sacrificial flame,
With sudden force to kindle a young nothingness
To new becoming of blessed poem,
—You sought me in your flaming abysses
And did not find me.

Then my messenger came to you
And placed your ear next to the still life of my earth,
Then you felt how seed after seed began to stir,
And all the movements of growing things encircled you,
Blood hammered against blood, and the silence overcame you,
The eternally complete, soft and motherly
—Then you had to incline upon yourself,
Then you found me.

DAS WORT AN ELIJAHU

Klagende sanken ins Grab
—Hör in den Lüften den Klang,—
Sprich, Menschensohn:
Ihr harrtet lang.

Dürstende sanken ins Grab
—Fühl allen Durst ungestillt,—
Sprich, Menschensohn:
Die Zeit ist erfüllt.

Segnende sanken ins Grab
—Sieh die erstarrte Gebärde,—
Sprich, Menschensohn:
Es werde!

THE WORD TO ELIJAH

They sank into the grave lamenting
—Hear in the air the clamor,—
Speak, son of man:
You are long in coming.

They sank into the grave thirsting
—Feel how all thirst is unquenched,—
Speak, son of man:
The time is fulfilled.

They sank into the grave blessing
—See the frozen gesture,—
Speak, son of man:
Let it become!

DER JÜNGER

Die graue Hand des Sturms lag über beiden.
Des Meisters Haar trug eine schwarze Glut.
Gehüllt und eingewiegt in stummes Leiden
War das Gesicht des Schülers, blass und gut.

Der Weg war felsig. Blitz und Bergesfeuer
Wob rings um sie ein zuckendes Geäst.
Des Knaben Schritt ward weich und immer scheuer,
Der Alte ging wie immer, grad und fest.

Die blauen Augen träumten zu den seinen,
Und durch die schmalen Wangen schlug die Scham,
Der Mund war starr wie von gepresstem Weinen,
Die grobe Sehnsucht eines Kindes kam.

Da sprach der Meister: "Von dem vielen Wandern
Nahm ich der einen Wahrheit goldne Macht:
Kannst du dein Eigen sein, sei nie des andern."
Und schweigend ging der Knabe in die Nacht.

THE DISCIPLE

The gray hand of the storm lay over both.
The Master's hair bore a black glow.
Enveloped and rocked to sleep in dumb suffering
Was the face of the disciple, pale and kind.

The way was rocky. Lightning and mountain fire
Zigzagged around them like trembling branches.
The boy's step grew weak and ever more timid,
The old man walked as always, straight and firmly.

The blue eyes gazed dreaming into his own,
And through the narrow cheeks beat the shame,
The mouth was set as from repressed weeping,
The great longing of a child came.

Then the master spoke: "From much wandering
I took the golden might of the one truth:
If you can be your own, never be another's."
And silently the boy walked in the night.

DIE MAGIER

Der Magier Schar zog an dem Herrn vorbei,
Der auf dem schwarzen Throne sass und schwieg.
Aus ihren langen magren Händen stieg
Der Duft der Nächte auf und zog vorbei.

Der eine sprach: Dem Glühn im Bergesschacht,
Dem winkend heissen Reifen erzner Frucht
Hab ich in treuem Schauen nachgesucht,
Und fand des Bildens Trieb im Bergesschacht.

Der andre sprach: Dem Blut des Samenkorns
Lauscht ich und hört es wachsen und wuchs mit,
In beiden war der Welle gleicher Schritt,
Ich fand des Werdens Kraft im Samenkorn.

So sprachen sie. Und andrer Rätselkunst
Erzählte viel von dunkler Zeichen Sinn.
Wortlos zog ein gekrönter Mann dahin.
Ihm ruft der Meister: "Sag uns deine Kunst!"

Der sprach, und jedes Herzens Schlag erstarb:
"Vor aller Macht ist mir der Drang geblieben
Nach einem Menschen, den ich möchte lieben.
Denn alle Macht ist tot." Das Wort erstarb.

THE MAGICIANS

The band of magicians marched by the master,
Who sat silently on the black throne.
From their long thin hands there arose
The fragrance of nights and marched by.

The one spoke: The glow in the mountain shaft,
Whose sparkling means the ripening of metal fruit
I have sought for in faithful beholding,
And found the drive to form in mountain shaft.

The other spoke: To the blood of the grain of seed
I listened and heard it grow and grew with it,
In both was the undulation of the same stride,
I found the force of becoming in the grain of seed.

Thus they spoke. And other riddle art
Told much of dark sign's sense.
A crowned man came thither wordlessly.
To him the master called: "Tell us your art!"

He spoke, and every heart's beat died away:
"Above all power there has remained to me
The craving for a man that I might love.
For all power is dead." The word died away.

GEWALT UND LIEBE

1

Unsre Hoffnung ist zu neu und zu alt—
Ich weiss nicht, was uns verbliebe,
Wäre Liebe nicht verklärte Gewalt
Und Gewalt nicht irrende Liebe.

2

Verschwör nicht: "Liebe herrsche allein!"
Magst du's bewähren?
Aber schwöre: An jedem Morgen
Will ich neu um die Grenze sorgen
Zwischen Liebestat-Ja und Gewalttat-Nein
Und vordringend die Wirklichkeit ehren.

3

Wir können nicht umhin,
Gewalt zu üben,
Dem Zwange nicht entfliehn,
Welt zu betrüben,
So lasst uns, Spruchs bedächtig
Und Widerspruches mächtig,
Gewaltig lieben.

POWER AND LOVE

1

Our hope is too new and too old—
I do not know what would remain to us
Were love not transfigured power
And power not straying love.

2

Do not protest: "Let love alone rule!"
Can you prove it true?
But resolve: Every morning
I shall concern myself anew about the boundary
Between the love-deed-Yes and the power-deed-No
And pressing forward honor reality.

3

We cannot avoid
Using power,
Cannot escape the compulsion
To afflict the world,
So let us, cautious in diction
And mighty in contradiction,
Love powerfully.

THE DEMONIC BOOK

THE BRETONS believe in the demonic book.

It has different names, one in each region. In that of Quimper it is called Ar Vif, that is, The Living.

It is a gigantic book. When it stands upright, it has the height of a man.

The pages are red, the letters are black.

But he who goes up to it and opens it sees nothing except red. The black signs only become visible when one has fought with the Vif and overpowered it.

For this book lives. And it will not let itself be questioned. Only he who conquers it tears from it its mystery.

He must labor with it hours at a time as with a headstrong horse, until covered with sweat he stands in front of it and reads this book that he has tamed.

It is a dangerous book. One fastens it up with a thick padlock and hangs it on a chain which is attached to the strongest beam. The beam must be warped.

He who has subdued the Vif knows the secret names of the demons and knows how to summon them.

He does not walk like all the world. He hesitates at every step, for he fears to tread on a soul. He has experienced something.

I think that every real book is Ar Vif.

The real reader knows this, but far better still the real writer—for only the writing of a real book is actually danger, battle, and overpowering. Many a one loses his courage midway, and the work that he began in the reading of the signs of the mystery he completes in the vain letters of his arbitrariness. There exists only a little reality of the spirit in this book-rich world.

AM TAG DER RUCKSCHAU

Der Schweifende sprach zu mir: Ich bin der Geist.
Die Schillernde sprach zu mir: Ich bin die Welt.
Er hatte mich mit Flügeln überkreist.
Sie hatte mich mit Flammenspiel umstellt.
Schon wollt ich ihnen fronen,
Schon war mein Herz genarrt,
Da trat vor die Dämonen
Eine Gegenwart.

Dem Schweifenden sagte sie: Du bist der Wahn.
Der Schillernden sagte sie: Du bist der Trug.
Da ward so Geist wie Welt mir aufgetan,
Die Lüge barst, und was war, war genug.
Du wirktest, dass ich schaue,—
Wirktest? du lebtest nur,
Du Element und Fraue,
Seele und Natur!

ON THE DAY OF LOOKING BACK

The roaming one spoke to me: I am the spirit.
The iridescent one spoke to me: I am the world.
He had hovered round me with wings.
She had encompassed me with play of flames.
Already I wanted to pander to them,
Already my heart was duped,
When there stepped before the demons
A presence.

To the roaming one it said: You are madness.
To the iridescent one it said: You are deception.
Then both spirit and world became open to me,
The lies burst, and what was, was enough.
You brought it about that I behold,—
Brought about? you only lived,
You element and woman,
Soul and nature!

WEISST DU ES NOCH...?

Weisst du es noch, wie wir in jungen Jahren
Mitsammen sind auf diesem Meer gefahren?
Gesichte kamen, gross und wunderlich,
Wir schauten miteinander, du und ich.
Wie fügte sich im Herzen Bild zu Bildern!
Wie stieg ein gegenseitig reges Schildern
Draus auf und lebte zwischen dir und mir!
Wir waren dort und waren doch ganz hier
Und gans beisammen, streifend und gegründet.
So ward die Stimme wach, die seither kündet
Und alte Herrlichkeit bezeugt als neu,
Sich selbst und dir und dem Mitsammen treu.
Nimm denn auch dieses Zeugnis in die Hände,
Es ist ein Ende und hat doch kein Ende,
Denn Ewiges hört ihm und hört uns zu,
Wie wir aus ihm ertönen, ich und du.

DO YOU STILL KNOW IT...?

Do you still know, how we in our young years
Traveled together on this sea?
Visions came, great and wonderful,
We beheld them together, you and I.
How image joined itself with images in our hearts!
How a mutual animated describing
Arose out of it and lived between you and me!
We were there and were yet wholly here
And wholly together, roaming and grounded.
Thus the voice awoke that since then proclaims
And witnesses to old majesty as new,
True to itself and you and to both together.
Take then this witness in your hands,
It is an end and yet has no end,
For something eternal listens to it and listens to us,
How we resound out of it, I and Thou.

SPIRITS AND MEN

IN THIS VOLUME* I have put together three books of tales by my wife who died in 1958 (maiden name: Paula Winkler, pen name: George Munk): *Die unechten Kinder Adams* (1912), *Sankt Gertrauden Minne* (1921), and *Die Gäste* (1927). They belong together. What makes them belong together I have tried to express in the title of this volume. Not all of these stories tell, to be sure, of that kind of creature that we are used to designate as a spirit. Yet they all bear witness to that wholly innerworldly mystery, accosting man in a natural way, indeed, the mystery that through this plural of "spirits" we can only barely do justice to. The—I repeat it—thoroughly natural phenomenon is formless, and it demands of us that we give it form, to do which, however, only poets, and even they only at times, are suited. The human accomplishment that is meant is usually ascribed to the "power of imagination," by which is implied that all that takes place here takes place in the sphere of the image-engendering psyche. The person to whom the like has happened knows otherwise. What met him, yes, met, he will not deny by enregistering it in a circle drawn by the hand of a psychology. But also he will not allow the so-called parapsychology to have a say in the matter. What meets him, indeed, is not objectively comprehensible outside of his own giving of form: it becomes an object through this giving of form and cannot become one except in this way. It exists within the world and

---

* Georg Munk, *Geister und Menschen* (Munich: Kösel-Verlag, 1961).

is independent of man and yet only through him capable of receiving form, just through the fact that it accosts him and awakens his power of formation, of composing. To create a story or poem means to fulfill the bidding of meetings, and within these meetings there are those of which I speak, those which lead to the composing of tales—not fairy tales, not romantic ghost stories, but genuine tales of spirits, reports of them, of spirits which in a special kind of natural mystery enter into our lives and perhaps abandon themselves to them.

In her youth Paula Winkler had already beheld the hidden reality that I mean, especially in the landscape of Southern Tyrol; childhood memories from the Bavarian forest also seem to have played their part. But that she could receive the mysterious, the alien to us that encountered her, without timidity, derived from the primal character of her being. She knew about the elemental from its own ground. There she was "the bold woman," who ventured upon the brokenness of the human house. Her receiving of the elemental, however, was precisely a formative one: not afterward, not in a willed elaboration of the experienced, not even in that unarbitrary activity of the formative memory did she lend form to the formless: she saw, she experienced it as form. And what then followed, when she wrote down something of it and thus presumed to hold it fast, was made possible by the fact that what she received, as it were, in an unextended moment she transposed into a course of time, gave it a history, told it. She was a narrating person, one of those to whom images become events and then the events become the course of a narrated life. From there she imparted to the elemental spirits, who know only cosmic, destiny-less time, our human time, that into which the dark threads of our afterknowledge of our birth are interwoven with the still darker threads of our foreknowledge of our death.

Not all, I have already said so, of the twelve tales that are united in this volume could be characterized as stories of spirits. But even those that do not belong to this category stem from meeting with that spiritual nature of the abysses that accost us from the midst of nature. Even where what is told is only of men the sphere of unifications opens itself to us.

A REALIST OF THE SPIRIT

WHEN I HEARD in 1905 that the Privatdozent in Theology, Albert Schweitzer, had begun to study medicine, I noticed it with interest, and when I heard eight years later that he had gone to the Congo not as a missionary but as a doctor in order to fight a serious sickness with which the natives were afflicted, the event assumed for me a positively symbolical character. I had become acquainted with Schweitzer in 1901 or 1902 through an essay of his on the mystery of the Last Supper. This essay made a deep impression on me because it brought Jesus into close relation with the mysteries of Jewish faith. At that time I had already called Schweitzer a theological realist because he saw the manifestations of the spirit in the context of the particular realities of faith in which they made their appearance. Now, with his study of medicine and his emigration to Lambarene, he proved by his own life that he was a realist of the spirit. To the realists whom I mean, men are not so fundamentally divided into body and soul that, when one wishes to help them, one may give one's attention exclusively to the soul. Where one is met by widespread bodily suffering to whose healing one believes oneself able to make an essential contribution, one feels oneself called to this task. The true doctor indeed has to do with body and soul in one, but the bodily suffering is manifest and it is with it that he must begin, though not without giving the soul a share in the process. If one approaches a doctor such as this, a man who is, to begin with, a theologian and who is destined to remain a theologian as long as he lives, and asks, "Must you not first of all concern yourself with the soul?" he answers, "The soul knows better how to wait than the body," and in saying this he remained, in fact, in the following of his master, who certainly did not begin again and again with the healing of bodily infirmities merely in order to give a sign.

Such was the manner of Schweitzer's working in the sphere of the participation of the spirit in life. But also in the sphere of spiritual work itself he remains the realist. His theological research has always been centrally concerned with the understanding of primitive Christianity as closely allied with the believing man's will toward the salvation of the world and the believing man's interpretation of the contemporary age as the aeon of salvation that has already begun. The spiritualized conception of redemption thus regained for Schweitzer its basic meaning, that of the factual salvation on earth of the whole human being.

But bound up with all this in addition is Schweitzer's philosophy, the leading idea of which is reverence for human life. This concept refers us once more to the body-soul totality of the individual living man as that which is to be actively honored and helped. Not only ethical but also political questions will be misunderstood if one thinks that one may deal with them as independent of the awesome reality of human living and dying.

Schweitzer's relation, as scholar and interpreter, to Bach, the great realist of the believing spirit, is also to be understood in its essence from this standpoint.

To us, before whose eyes spirit and life have fallen apart from each other more radically perhaps than in any earlier time, it is a great comfort and encouragement that this man exists, in whom their created togetherness is manifested and confirmed.

MEMORIES OF HAMMARSKJOLD

I HAVE been asked to say something about myself to the listeners of the Swedish Radio. Still it would probably be best if I tell you of my relations to a great son of the Swedish people, Dag Hammarskjøld.

When in the spring of 1958 I delivered guest lectures at Princeton University, Hammarskjøld wrote me that he had read in my book *Pointing the Way* my addresses and essays on the basic political problems of this hour. "I want to tell you," he wrote, "how strongly I have responded to what you write about our age of distrust and to the background of your observations which I find in your philosophy of unity created 'out of the manifold.'" When we then met in the house of the organization so remarkably named the United Nations, it proved to be the case that both of us were indeed concerned about the same thing: he who stood in the most exposed position of international responsibility, I who stand in the loneliness of a spiritual tower, which is in reality a watchtower from which all the distances and depths of the planetary crisis can be descried. That we were concerned, I say, about the same thing. We were both pained in the same way by the pseudo-speaking of representatives of states and groups of states who, permeated by a fundamental reciprocal mistrust, talked past one another out the windows. We both hoped, we both believed that still in sufficient time before the catastrophe, faithful representatives of the people, faithful to their mission, would enter into a genuine dialogue, a genuine dealing with one another out of which would emerge in all clarity the fact that the common interests of the peoples were stronger still

than those which kept them in opposition to one another. A
genuine dealing with one another in which it must occur that
a working together—I do not say, a coexistence, that is not
enough, I say and mean, despite all the monstrous difficulties,
a cooperation—must be preferred to the common destruction. For there is no third possibility, only one of these two:
common realization of the great common interests or the end
of all that on the one side and the other one is accustomed to
call civilization. At that time, in the house of the United Nations, sitting across from each other, we both recognized, Dag
Hammarskjøld and I, what it was essentially that bound us to
each other. But I sensed, looking at and listening to him,
something else that I could not explain to myself, something
fateful that in some way was connected with his function in
this world-hour.

Soon thereafter, in June 1958, in a speech of thanks to
Cambridge University for the honorary doctorate that they
had conferred upon him, he bore witness to what we had in
common by quoting with especial emphasis a large part of
the address that I had delivered in New York in 1952, and
indeed that part the subject of which was the fighting of the
general existential mistrust.

In January 1959 Hammarskjøld visited me in Jerusalem.
In the center of our conversation stood the problem that has
ever again laid claim to me in the course of my life: the failure of the spiritual man in his historical undertakings. I illus-
trated it by one of the highest of the examples that have
become known to us: the abortive attempt of Plato to establish his just state in Sicily. I felt, and Hammarskjøld—of that
I was certain—also felt as I did, we too were the recipients of
that letter in which Plato tells of his failure and of his overcoming his failure.

In August 1961 Hammarskjøld wrote me about his impressions on reading one of my philosophical works. He
would, he wrote, translate some of these books into Swedish,
"so as to bring you closer to my countrymen," he added and

asked which book I held to be the most suitable. In my answer I recommended to him that he translate the book *I and Thou*. He went to work immediately. In the letter in which he informed me of this, he described this book as the "key work," "decisive in its message." I received that letter an hour after I had heard the news of his death on the radio. As was later reported to me, even on his last flight he was working on the translation of *I and Thou*.

ON LEO SHESTOV

SHESTOV IS one of the representative thinkers of our epoch. He is a questioning thinker. But not like Socrates, who knows the right answer and at first "ironically" withholds it from his partner in dialogue. Shestov has no finished answers in his pocket; but he knows what is to be asked today and here; he teaches us to ask. In so doing he does not shy away at times from finding two answers that contradict each other instead of a single one. He has himself (in a notation that is superscribed "Pro domo") pointed out that he is accustomed to speak of such contradictions openly. But thereby he teaches us something very important for us contemporary men: that one may not overcome such contradictions prematurely—and that means seemingly.

It is this unfrightened honesty of his questioning that has made Shestov the eminent religious thinker that he is.

ON RICHARD BEER-HOFMANN

THERE ARE poets who in their poetic way and work are determined by a basic motif that changes and in changing grows. Such a poet was Richard Beer-Hofmann. A foreword to the collected edition of his works is assigned the task of indicating his basic motif and its transformations.

It is the motif of death. It is common, to be sure, to him and to other German-language poets of his time and atmosphere, especially the Austrian poets, and among these above all the Jews, among whom we may place here an individual who descends from the Jewish people in one line of his ancestry—I mean Hofmannsthal. The Vienna circle to which he and Beer-Hofmann belonged also included Schnitzler. The death motif does not appear here as the subject of a single author, as later in the work of Kafka and in that of Broch; it is as if to the circle bound by friendship is lent another special, specially formed common element. It was Schnitzler who sought to explain this element when he wrote, "A presentiment of the end of their world blows around them . . . for the end of their world is near." One knows how great a place dying and being dead occupy in Schnitzler's work, especially in his stories. That presentiment does not become evident here just as little as it does among the works of his friends; nonetheless, it is important for our understanding that it is testified to as a dynamic.

For Schnitzler, who wants to tell of individual destinies, death is the most elemental expression of personal destiny: the universal primal question which is posed by its factuality is here hardly perceptible. It is that which Hofmannsthal

61

places before our eyes, already in 1893 when he sees death in the glorification customary in antiquity, and even in 1922 when he points to it in blunt harshness, as he bids him whom he has accosted—whether poet or reader—"to leave the stage."

Almost nowhere are we allowed to think here of a relative overcoming of the fact of death. Yet there resounds at times, most clearly in the young Hofmannsthal (1894), the theme of the "forebears" as a motif of duration, of enduring. It is this theme to gain possession of which Richard Beer-Hofmann so struggled that no victory could satisfy him until he was able to see into and fathom the depths. From then on he developed it to its own characteristic form, the completion of which death denied to the poet, wrestling long and hard with his work, and to his readers.

It is undoubtedly the unfolding of the forces preparing themselves for such a struggling and growing in Beer-Hofmann's soul that moved the twenty-three-year-old Hofmannsthal to write to his older friend he knew with certainty "that there is no man to whom I am so indebted as I am to you." That was 1897, in the very year in which Beer-Hofmann wrote the "Schlaflied an Miriam" ("Lullaby for Miriam") with which he concluded the first stage of his struggles for the answer to death.

The first expression of this struggle we find four years earlier in the artistically still unsure story "The Child." The death that is told of here is decidedly not a greater God of the soul as for Hofmannsthal in the same period; it *is* not at all, it merely happens, crassly incidental. What takes place is the simply absurd, the dying of a child. That his father submits to this death without experiencing it as reality, that he later only attains to the threshold of this reality, allows us, along with all the abstractness of the development, to note: here is the beginning of a way.

The "Lullaby," the first testimony of poetic maturity, is at the same time the first answer of Beer-Hofmann to the fact

of death. The child in the cradle is addressed as the creature
who still knows nothing about death. It will someday experience what it is, come to feel what the poet in this moment
feels: "No one can be an heir to anyone here." (Here too it
may prove fruitful to compare the perhaps contemporary
poem of Hofmannsthal on the "Heir" who "smiles when the
innermost recesses of life whisper: death!") But now the insight develops unexpectedly in the heart of the father. Our
being itself is an inheritance from our forebears that we be-
queath to our children. The feeling that we are endangered
has deceived us. If "all" are really "in us," then the terror of
loneliness is forever banished: death has become a servant of
life.

Three years before, a year after that poem about the
"Heir," this motif was sounded in Hofmannsthal's "Terzi-
nen," where he says of his forebears (on both sides) that they
are as at one with him as his own hair. Thus at that time,
1894, the view of our ending and our new beginning had become common to the friends—in which the older one con-
ceptually, if not poetically, took the lead.

Three years after the "Lullaby" the strange book *The
Death of George* (*Der Tod Georgs*) appeared, which in seemingly narrative but basically almost anti-epic form strung
together meditations on the significance of the fact of death
in the life of a living person. We encounter dying here in
three spheres of existence: as the dream of the death of a
woman who is familiar to the sleeper as his wife but who
"had never lived"; as the fantasy picture of sacral orgies in a
Syrian temple that issue into death; and as the simple reality
of lived life: the death of a friend (friend? At this point the
complaint of the "Lullaby," "No one can be a companion to
anyone here" is resumed); "the real death" which awakens in
the survivors the painful observation of the passing and passing away of personal existence—first an insight into the guilt
of "arrogance," then insight into the law of "righteousness."
And now, at the end of the book, there appears again that

motif of the forebears from the "Lullaby." But now it is no longer something almost universal as before ("Blood of our fathers, full of unrest and pride"): it is something entirely definite, historically unique. "Above the life of those," it reads here, "whose blood flowed in him righteousness" stood like a sun, and it had called "to God the righteous" "a people chosen for suffering" in their age-long torments. It is Israel that is being spoken of. In the hour in which Beer-Hofmann prepared himself to set down this conclusion of his first real work he must have recognized the special poetic task that had been set him. The almost playful image that appears in the first part of the book of a sun shedding its blood in golden rays as the way in which the longed-for "free splendid death" appears to him, is expelled into the realm of glittering nothingness to which it belongs by the true counterimage, the image of the martyrdom of a people.

But now Beer-Hofmann's way veers, and to him who would follow it step by step it must now seem, for a good long while, that that answer to the fact of death that had only just been begun in the "Lullaby," in *The Death of George* would not come to completion. For what the next work, the tragedy *The Count of Charolais* (1905), has to say to us, beyond all action and speech, is precisely this, that no answer to death exists. The drama begins with death already having occurred, with the fate of a corpse; it ends with this same man, who fought over the corpse of his father, driving his beloved wife to her death. The playwright has, to be sure, said of his piece that in it he had "written the tragedy to the end." But that is valid only for the modern tragedy stemming from the Elizabethan which affords no answer to death, not for the ancient tragedy which again and again allowed a speech of reconciliation of a god to follow the human end. And had Beer-Hofmann been permitted to write the last part of his work of old age, the David trilogy, to which he had intended giving the title "The Death of David," then death would not have been tragic here in the modern sense, but it also would no longer have needed any epiphany, for everything of the trilogy which has taken form in words bears in itself the answer to death. And this answer is the clarification and completion of what had only just been intimated in the "Lullaby," what in the final section of *The Death of George* had found a clarifying but not yet a definitive expression. But now the way of the poet was diverted from the task of giving an adequate form to this answer. The poem "Aging" ("*Altern*") published shortly afterward (1906) solves the riddle, to be sure, only in such a way that from the mystery something new, forever puzzling arises. The ground of a later reality is cut from under this connection with the forebears, formerly praised by the poet. For here in a statement that sounds like the poetizing of a great but incomplete insight of Kant's, it says:

> Space, like time: spun web, ghosts
> Which the senses have woven around you!

Death and life, so we are told, are only prisons in which we have walled ourselves: we should break them and step forth into freedom where "the clear air showers around" us. Here the presentiment of eternity is spoken of, a clear presentiment but one that removes us from all warmth of earth—the eternity of the primal ground out of which time and space arise. These two prove themselves, indeed, when we wish to take them as ultimate realities, as inconceivable to the point of absurdity, no matter whether we seek to imagine them as finite or as infinite: only as borne by a timeless and spaceless eternity are they comprehensible.

The vital connection with the ancestors and the presentiment—only hovering around us, to be sure, but nonetheless reliable—of an eternity above time, belong together like the systole and the diastole. Only he who knows the twofold answer to death, that which arises out of our reality and that which can only be glimpsed, this side of death, only he who knows both in one knows the answer.

The poet's turning away from the comforting knowledge of the connection with the ancestors has taken a wholly empirical form in *The Count of Charolais,* in the poem "Aging" a transcendental one: there death rules as one who admits no answer, here an inner certainty reaches beyond its so massive factuality—not the certainty of a continuation in time but of the final entrance into the eternity that is already present now and always. It is as if that only represented and not spoken No had demanded that this poetically directly spoken Yes follow it. In the biographical occurrence of the turning away from that consolation, genuinely felt and full chorded but inadequate in the face of existence, the two belong together.

For the sake of understanding this inner connection, however, a passage must be pointed out here in the major work of that period, the *Count of Charolais,* the action of which takes place "many centuries ago." What is meant is the scene in which "the red Itzig" adds, as it were, what Shylock left unsaid about the ignominy of Jewish existence in the Christian world. One may suppose that what is expressed here is something by which Beer-Hofmann was deeply struck at the time: the insight into how much there was intermixed in the "unrest and pride" of the blood of the fathers the experience of the injuries that had been done to them in body and soul— done to them under the eyes of God.

Here, in my opinion, the great search for meaning was inserted into the way of the poet. It is from the standpoint of this search that we can understand what now followed: the turning back to the past which is so decisive for Beer-Hofmann's later work. This turning back is not a mere resumption of the theme of the forebears, as it might appear. That theme now becomes a framework in which we encounter for the first time an image, *the* image, the meaning-filled image of an Israel that suffers for God's sake as his witness, that becomes through this suffering the "light of the peoples" and overcomes the death of a people.

On this foundation of rock Beer-Hofmann wanted to construct his David trilogy, of which he was only able to finish the prelude and the first part.

In the prelude, *Jacob's Dream,* a theme is unfolded in high pathos, a pathos which even at the greatest height remains legitimate. The Biblical subject is transformed here, but the transformation takes place in genuine faithfulness, the faithfulness of the late-born who has found what he is permitted to say in the search for a poetically expressible meaning.

"He called me from the womb," it says (Isaiah 49:2) in the speech of God in Deutero-Isaiah from which Beer-Hofmann took some sentences to set as a motto at the head of his poem. The summons and election of the father of the tribe is announced to him in a dream. This election means task and destiny but not inevitable fate. In his, Jacob's, own decision the destiny is established: he may choose this election, he may reject it. And what it means is not concealed from him. He, his seed, to be sure, as it says in that speech of God, will be given as a light to the tribes of the world, but they will respond to what he does for them by spitting in his face. "Where could one find the insult that will not happen to you?" says Samael, the demon afflicted by God, to Jacob (we think of the speech of the red Itzig), and further: "They scourge you . . . He permits it." The angels standing around accuse Samael of lying, but God himself confirms: Yes, this task is bound up with this destiny, and grace will only stream to those who have passed through it faithfully. And now, knowing, Jacob chooses this election.

That Jacob decides thus is to be understood from the fact that the essential out of which alone that "light" can come lives in his innermost heart. It is love—the gracious love of God for men and the active love of man for his fellowman, indeed, for all existing beings, but above all for those who are dependent upon him and are thus entrusted to him. One reads how Jacob lovingly gave water to and cared for the lamb; and here one may reach from the work of the poet into his own life that followed later and think of what we learn of his relationship to an animal from his "Song to the Dog Ardon" and the story of his death (in the book *Paula*). One reads with what loving gestures Jacob emancipated the slave Idnibaal into freedom; and again the reader may step over into the biographical realm and remember what is told him (again in the book *Paula*) of the relation of the family to the servant Vinzek. But it is necessary to understand that for Jacob in the dependence of that being upon him is mirrored his own creaturely dependence upon God, in Idnibaal's trust in him his own "blessed trust" in God. The young David knows it: "The world stands on trust." Already in Jacob's heart the love that he practices toward others and the love that he still receives from God in every suffering are inseparably united.

One may call to mind here the bond that joins the two statements about love in the Deuteronomic teaching, "God, . . . who loves the stranger" and, "So love then the stranger."

In the concluding section of the book *The Death of George* we read how the survivor, Paul, attains to the insight that once "above the life of those whose blood flowed in him," stood "righteousness like a sun," a sun "whose rays did not warm them" and to which they nonetheless adhered. In *Jacob's Dream,* too, we hear of the righteousness of God which Jacob and his people have to proclaim. But the central message of this work is that of the other sun of love that warms throughout the world: the love of God for his creatures, the love of man for both—his love for God "as He is, cruel and merciful," his love for his suffering fellow creatures. That is the message of the ancestors which is inborn in their descendants, to hearken to which signifies the ever renewed overcoming of death in its most threatening form, the death of the people.

Of the trilogy to which this is the prelude we have only the first part and the prologue to the second. Still we can reconstruct for ourselves the central theme of the work, namely, that that which in the prelude announced itself only in the form of a personal existence, the meaning of which fore-shadowed that of people, state, history—the life of the "chosen" man, in his faithful partnership with God and with the creature, should fulfill itself here in the dimension of history. In the single completed part of the trilogy, "The Young David," which deals with the *development* of the historical situation, we can only glimpse this—particularly in the testimony of the daily companions of David. More than this is not given to us. The poet may not disavow the hard Biblical report concerning David's life. In the "Prelude in the Theater" of "King David" we are clearly told that the drama will portray a David who in many respects is more like the alien kings from the history of the peoples than the prehistorical father of the tribe. What is essential here is the fulfillment in spite of all, in going through. Above all going through the chasm of guilt into which the forefathers had not set foot; the middle part of the trilogy is devoted to presenting this guilt and its atonement. Devoted to, not imposed! For in no other way than this can the great ruler become the great praying man whose image is transmitted to us: those psalms which sound most genuine are precisely those in which God is implored for "cleansing." The prologue of the poet who speaks in the "Prelude in the Theater," praises David as "blessed, sinful." For thus the poet Richard Beer-Hofmann saw David's way to death: from the grace of the election through sin to that higher grace which is only granted to those who have turned.

HERMANN HESSE'S
SERVICE TO THE SPIRIT

Asked to speak on the eightieth birthday of my friend Hermann Hesse, I felt and explained that I could not do what is expected at such an event: an evaluation of his total creative works. What I believed myself able to do and therefore undertook is a pointing to the significance that the central section of these works, the series of great novels beginning in Hesse's Schwabian period, assumes within the strivings of our time concerning the position of the spirit. From them a personal way, piece by piece of this way, can be made exemplarily visible.

That it is narrative works with which we are concerned must be understood as essential. The writer who is called to be a narrator experiences and reports all being as occurrence. Landscape, conceptual expression, yes even the movements of the soul are communicated to us here as unbroken event. When Hesse in 1917, after some delightful narrative books which had been joyfully received as such, entered into the service of the spirit, he had to narrate as bodily occurrences an idea of the spirit which he had experienced from the spirit in the sphere of bodily occurrences. In the middle of his life the hand of the spirit had torn the poet Hesse out of carefree storytelling and compelled him to report his, the spirit's wrestling, its dangers and risks, epically, that is as events of the life of man with man. Through this his concern became from work to work in an ever more exact sense a spiritual one. But at the same time his narrative mastery perfected itself, the power of transforming problem into event. Finally, when what was to be reported was an imaginary realm of the spirit enclosed within itself, no other language was perceptible than that of the happening. The destiny of the spirit became manifest as a process unfolded to our senses.

2

The destiny of the spirit—in our age what is meant by that is above all the crisis of the spirit, more exactly: the crisis in its relation to life. In the heaven of philosophy the signs of this crisis had already announced themselves previously. Overpowered by storming and demanding life, the spirit contested its own office as the finder of truth and the speaker of law, it set life free and wanted now only to be its interpreter, depending on the circumstances, a dithyrambic or even a pragmatically teaching interpreter. What the emancipated life would do with its freedom, that we have fully experienced since then. But before this manifested itself unmistakably, the resonance of life resounded to the call of the spirit; rather, it was now the creative spirit which spoke in the name of the unbound life, rebelled against the tyranny of an absolute morality and glorified the sovereign individuation. The first in the series of works of Hermann Hesse that mirror the life of the spirit belongs here, that inflammatory *Demian* from the time of the First World War, in which the rights of a sovereign Cain are asserted against an obsequious Abel—an attitude which even in Byron's time was already a prerogative of the poet longing for freedom from law.

It is no accident that Hesse supplemented this anthropological postulate by a theological one, and that the God that he proclaimed was none other than that gnosticizing being Abraxas that we also encounter in an early writing of the psychologist Carl Gustav Jung. This being, as Hesse says, "has the symbolic task of uniting the divine and the diabolical," and thus possesses in eternal fullness that very thing which the psychological teaching of its adepts calls accomplishing the integration of the evil.

It appears as though what arose here was only a rebellion against the power of the *creator spiritus* which does not merely distinguish between light and darkness but also presently between holy and profane. And yet with this first work of the series the poet Hesse's service of the spirit begins. For the way of the human spirit commences ever again with a daring breakthrough, and every breakthrough is preceded by an audacious rupture. Everything depends upon the direction which is now taken. One cannot go back, and one may not remain standing there where one has reached, for he who remains in the rupture forfeits the life of the spirit. In the search for the living God one must now and again destroy the images that have become unworthy in order to create room for a new one. But the Abraxas is no image of God at all but a complex concept, the concept of a fusion of good and evil of ultimate validity. One must turn one's back on it if one wants to go forward. For a being that simply represents and legitimizes ourselves, elevated into the unconditional, is not of a divine nature.

After the breakthrough of *Demian* Hesse was not bent on a reconciliation. He has remained on the side of rebelling life. But the next step led him to a rung of greater illumination.

3

The next novel in the series, *Siddhartha,* which is described as "Indian fiction" and stems from the first years after the war, gives a new and significant form to the great question that runs through all of these works of Hesse's, the question of the goal of the spirit.

Siddhartha, a contemporary of the Buddha, resists the teaching of the master because, like all teaching, it is one-sided. He, Siddhartha, rejects all teachings, which necessarily affirm one thing and deny another, for they cannot, in his opinion, do justice to the reality of existing being. He, Siddhartha, does not want to fathom and split the world, the real world, in which sin and grace dwell close together, through Yes and No, but only to love it, to love it as just what it is, existing in itself.

In *Demian* Hesse had represented the demand of pressing life against the dictates of the spirit; in *Siddhartha* no longer is any demand made. There the goal was perfect individuation, here it was the love for the world irreproachable in its continuance. Here as there the spirit finally stands against the spirit, but there for the sake of release of the elemental forces that were repressed by the spirit, here for its own, the spirit's sake in order that what it may love in the world and what it has to despise should no longer be prescribed. Between that world and this one stands the beginning of the cruel lesson of the age: that life, when it is no longer obedient to the spirit, rages against itself and destroys itself. Siddhartha may in a fixed meditation embrace sin and grace as one: when he no longer has to do with the general essence "sin" but perhaps with the actual deed of violence that rises before his eyes, with the mistreatment of the weak by the strong, with the exploitation of the dependent by those who have power over them, he, Siddhartha, will forget the all-love and take up his stand against evil. In the dimension of the factual, in order that human evil not become overwhelming, the spirit must time after time distinguish within the human world as forcefully as it is at times able to do. The man Hesse has himself indeed become ever more directly acqainted with this critical state of the world-loving man and, in an age in which the spiritual have in so many different ways made themselves the slaves of the holders of power, has fearlessly confirmed the spirit's free holding of its ground.

4

The book *Steppenwolf* that now follows in the series belongs only peripherally to the theme of the service of the spirit. For all its unreserved modernity still a deeply romantic work, it goes back in a strange way to the phase of the rupture. It is as though the author had felt himself hindered in ascending further by something which, although of basic importance at that time, a decade before, remained unsaid. The book should be understood as the "inner biography" of a man who, as Hesse says, "is already defined as a nonbourgeois by his grade of individuation." *Siddhartha* had already led a significant step beyond this basic view, but, as it were, over something that now demanded to be borne along, to be recovered.

5

But immediately after this intermezzo appassionato we are already given a new rung to climb.

*Narziss and Goldmund,** a hard and basically melancholy work, is in this series the most polished, the roundest narrative in the sense of the classical tradition. In contrast to the earlier books of the sequence, the rebellious spirit which is incarnated in the chief character is accompanied by a counterpart of equal value, and between the two of them—between the spirit which is ever anew at the point of starting out, roving, vehemently grasping and what is thus grasped shaping into image, and the ascetic spirit, devoted to thought, answering life with the idea—there prevails a grandly conceived dialogical relationship. Within both the authenticity of the spirit dwells, both are spirit, both together are the spirit. Here first Hesse has given bodily form to the conflict of the spirit, in the duality of these two men who do not fight against each other but are rather there opposite each other and just in this way *with* each other. The thinker Narziss is wrong, therefore, when he says to his antagonist and friend, the sculptor Goldmund, speaking about his own kind, that spirit cannot live in nature, only against it, as its opponent.

---

* Hermann Hesse. *Narziss and Goldmund* (New York: Harper & Row, 1966)—M.F.

Only both together, the one who submits to nature and the one who resists it, both together are the spirit. The conflict of the spirit—which in history, working together with historical factors in a characteristic fashion, ever again explodes into crises—is here comprehended and reported in the image of two men being opposite and with each other.

Only the life of the one, the artist, is really narrated, to be sure. The monk Narziss speaks to us, but he remains throughout it all as if impassive; we barely learn what happens to him. Hesse later profoundly recognized how he had been guilty toward the thinking spirit, and in the last work of the series, *Magister Ludi,* he provided a great compensation for it.

In another notable respect that especially concerns us here, in *Narziss and Goldmund* a bridge was constructed, as it were, to the much later *Magister Ludi.* Narziss says of himself, "The goal is this: always to place myself there where I can best serve . . . Within that which is possible to me, I will serve the spirit as I understand it." To this there corresponds on the next higher rung that mysterious fact that Leo, the "servant" of the League of Eastern Wayfarers, reveals himself as its highest master, and also even in the name of Joseph Knecht, whose life story is told in *Magister Ludi,* there sounds forth the same motif.* The law that rules here is called by Leo "the law of service."

6

In these last two works of the series, the theme that has been developed in the earlier ones, that of the conflict of the spirit, seems no longer to be present. The spirit neither fights here for the right of life nor sets the all-affirming life against the distinctions of knowledge, nor, in the shape of two persons, is the adventurous and image-rich spirit opposed to the self-contained one. And yet the communal reality that *The*

---

* *Knecht* in German means servant—M.F.

Journey to the East documents and the great peace that prevails in *Magister Ludi* could certainly not have been attained
otherwise than in striding through the fire of the opposites,
and in the heart of the Journey and the Bead Game the transformed fire continues to glow.

The fantastic parable of the Journey to the East, executed
in a late romanticism rich in humor yet in its core entirely of
our time, is the successful attempt to grasp and narrate as one
common journey the dream journeys of all men who possess
a strongly imaged power of wish. I call it a successful attempt
because Hesse has succeeded in reporting as just one occurrence this inconceivable voyage simultaneously through space
and times, voyage of a great band and yet at the same time in
subgroups of those who belong together more closely, but
finally of each individual toward the unattainable goal of his
life wish.

The band consists not only of contemporary living men but
also of heroes of the ages enwoven in saga; to the historical
figures are joined figures of ancient and modern epics, and
even pseudonyms of Hermann Hesse dare to mingle in the
midst of them. They are all united in one "league," the
League of the Eastern Wayfarers, who travel separately and
together toward their goal, the land of the wishes infused by
the power of their imagination. This impossible and yet real
league-like unity has replaced the struggling solitudes of those
preceding novels of Hesse's. With this league and this order,
which bear the happenings here and in *Magister Ludi,* the
category of "We" is included in Hesse's work. Accordingly
the turning point of the story of the Journey to the East comes
when the League member who is telling it, designated without any pseudonym as "H. H.," falls prey to doubt concerning the reality of the League, and the way in which he re-
gains the belief and thereby the reality itself on a higher
level is its high point. It is the reality of the spirit which builds
worlds out of the world, and this spirit is in the final ground
a communal one.

The Journey to the East does not have a real ending. The narrator breaks off; and yet the faithful reader does not experience this conclusion as fragmentary. The double figure that we are given to see out of a "half-real" H. H. and a wholly real Leo lets us feel fully how the spirit journeys through flesh and blood into the image-work. The narration has fulfilled what it was obliged to as a confession, and has thereby become a parable.

7

One may regard *The Journey to the East* as a prelude to the last and most important work of the series, *Magister Ludi*. In neither can we discover anything of that storming of the spirit that raged through the earlier works. But in *The Journey to the East* it is still the failure of man in the tests of the spirit that is described; in *Magister Ludi* a great peace reigns between both. What takes place here takes place in the long familiar dimensions of human existence, even though in a future phase of development of this existence; and yet it delights us as though the spirit which has taken shelter in man was its own guest.

The spirit's being at home with itself, its communion with itself, has taken here the form of a game; and not otherwise than in this form could the facts of the spirit be narrated in so composed a manner. It is this game which does not reach out beyond itself but follows its own strict law, this completely regulated game "with the total contents and values of our culture," equally related to music and to mathematics, art and science at the same time, this perfecting of *homo ludens* out of the most extreme high discipline of the spirit, that the Castalian Order of the Bead Players serves. This is the order which has installed Joseph Knecht as Magister Ludi. Knecht works for this spirit in this its late form with a great, never-slackening devotion and in a serenity that nothing can trouble. He succeeds in bringing the educational work of the order to still greater perfection. At the same time it dawns in him ever more clearly and inexorably that with all this the responsibility of the spirit for the world of living and suffering men entrusted to it is rather avoided than fulfilled. The spirit is summoned as helper of the infinitely surrendered and by itself infinitely threatened life, and one serves it badly when one does not provide the help that it has to offer life. Joseph Knecht gives up his office and leaves the order with the intention of beginning anew as teacher in an ordinary school somewhere in the land. First of all, he wants to tutor the son of a friend. In order to win the full trust of the youth, he follows him in a precarious swimming race and drowns. When I read this conclusion of the splendidly executed book, I am touched each time in a strange fashion by the conception of the sacrificial death, which in Knecht's story of an imaginary earlier incarnation the rain maker of a matriarchal tribe takes on himself because he has not averted a cosmic catastrophe.

8

The spirit has not arisen as a wonderful byproduct of the evolving process of nature; it has appeared on his way to a wonderful natural being, called man, and has entered into him. Paracelsus and following him a poet of our time, Hofmannsthal, know to say of it that it does not dwell in us. I believe, rather, that it does and does not dwell in us. We are indebted to it for Promethean gifts, and it has suffered like Prometheus. In order to help the life of man, it has fought against all kinds of monstrous things. But it has collapsed into itself and has made war on itself, and since then it can no longer be for us a competent helper. We have fallen into great need, it has stood by us, and it has betrayed us, for it was no longer a whole and united spirit. Today it stands in crisis. Its crisis is ours. It can only become whole and united when it stakes itself for our unity.

Hermann Hesse has served the spirit through the fact that

he, as the storyteller that he is, has told of the contradiction between spirit and life and of the conflict of the spirit against itself. In this way he has made more visible the obstacle-ridden path that can lead to a new wholeness and unity. But as the man that he is, as the *homo humanus* that he is, he has performed the same service through the fact that he always, where it was valid, interceded for the wholeness and unity of the human being.

It is not the League of Eastern Wayfarers and the Bead Players alone who greet you today in all the world, Hermann Hesse. The servants of the spirit in all the world call out together a great greeting of love to you. Everywhere where one serves the spirit, you are loved.

AUTHENTIC BILINGUALISM

THE SYMBIOSIS of the German and the Jewish spirits brought forth in its final decades a series of poets who deserve a special attention, especially as regards the manner in which the mixtures and separations of these two determining powers of the soul are manifested in their work. Three categories can be distinguished here without difficulty. In the first the Jewish element can be recognized by the attentive receiver as something penetrating to him from the ground of the poem but hardly accessible to comparative analysis; it is incontestably there, but as soon as one tries to classify it, it escapes. The second category is characterized by the fact that the Jewish element also rules here as motif; Jewish, indeed primal Jewish motifs, appear here not as mere special moods, but as special movements; they penetrate the poem, they stamp it, indeed one may at times say that it is just these motifs that have engendered it. There is, however, a third kind. In the sphere of German poetry it cannot be distinguished from the first two; but there destiny and inspiration drive the poet, drive a part of his work beyond the German language: he remains faithful to it, he says in it what he has to say in it, but in order to express another reality that has fatefully approached him, he must enter another, hereditary sphere, must now also—I emphasize both "must" and "also" —compose poetry in his hereditary language. This third category is represented by one single poet of a high rank, Ludwig Strauss.

One may by no means regard the fact that after his immigration to Palestine Strauss wrote Hebrew poetry as some-

80

thing important in his life but not to be discussed in this place, at the beginning of a collected edition of his German work. For this special bilingualism, Strauss's Palestinian further poetizing in German and his new poetizing in Hebrew are representative for a significant situation in the history of the spirit, for the exodus of the Jewish spirit from the German culture. What this exodus means for German culture does not belong here; but its effect on the existence and work of the generations who made the exodus—only these and not those born later—this must here, just here be indicated.

Strauss's active inclination toward Yiddish may be regarded by the friend who survives him as a prelude, as it were, to this turning point in his poetical history. Yiddish is that spoken idiom of the popular masses of East European Jewry that has ever again delighted me as the popular itself become speech. Ludwig Strauss, the Rhenish Jew in whose soul the Rhine had rooted itself, loved the Polish Jew with a not at all arbitrary, not at all programmatic, with a simple, spontaneous love. This love put it into his mind to translate Yiddish folk songs.*

The Yiddish idiom that developed in the East out of the Jewish-German dialect has (along with many Hebrew and a few Slavic colorations) preserved the German speech culture. The Yiddish folk song—as Strauss emphasized in his foreword to the second of his collections of songs written down in Munich in January 1935—had been strongly influenced by the German. The wanderer from the German exile brought with him into East Europe German spiritual treasure fused with his own.

When at the beginning of 1935 Strauss emigrated from the Germany of Adolf Hitler to the Palestinian original homeland, he entered into a community in which, together with the centering migration from which it stemmed, a most re-

---

* These translations were published in two little volumes: *Ostjüdische Liebeslieder* (Berlin: Welt-Verlag, 1920) and *Jüdische Volkslieder* (Berlin: Schocken Verlag, 1935).

markable transformation took place: an ancient tongue which had been maintained for millenia in the atmosphere of will, essentially in cult and study, became spoken again, became again natural and self-understood. The multitudes from very different realms of speech who assembled here entered into a synthetic process, into the coming to be of a shared spontaneity of the tongue. Such a process can only be completed in the course of generations. Yet there are already many there who did not speak Hebrew because they determined to do so but because the very tongue itself fatefully took possession of their corporeality, because it fatefully emanated from their brain and their throat. The men who spontaneously thought in Hebrew were the true beginners here in this land. But a special place in the history of this incarnation of the spirit is occupied by those men who, likewise not arbitrarily but out of necessity, began to write poetry in Hebrew. Among them, however, Ludwig Strauss holds a place of his own: because here, in the newly won homeland, a long while after he had begun—compelled by the destiny of the heart—to write poetry in Hebrew, he continued to write German poetry— both in fully valid authenticity.

This phenomenon of bilingualism is utterly different from that with which we are familiar, particularly through Rilke's French poetry. These latter proceed from an artistic mastery which, as is well known, Rilke only late brought under the domination of a higher power; here, in the French poems, this artistic mastery rules without opposition, manipulating the modern form of the French lyric almost as if in play. Strauss's poetic bilingualism means the domination of destiny, of landscape and the developing people, in the depths from which the word ascends. He himself has twice in *Fahrt and Erfahrung* [*Journey and Experience*], in the section "An die Bucht" ["In the Bay"] and at the beginning of the section "Billige Reime" ["Cheap Rhymes"], undertaken to make clear to himself and his reader what was in question here. We hear here of a still earlier "instinctive attempt" "to say in Hebrew" what he "had wanted to say in German"; we hear from a later period that he had succeeded in saying much in Hebrew that "German would not have allowed to come to words" for him. What happened there was expressed still more forcefully in an untranslatable pair of Hebrew verses. It is untranslatable because it plays with the double sense of a Hebrew noun that means both lip and language. "Where is the language [lip]," asks Strauss, "in which I can say all that is in me? My two languages [lips] are the pair of lips of my heart."

For what concerns us here, however, a still stronger, direct testimony is accessible when we compare with each other the German and the Hebrew versions of the first of the only two poems that Strauss wrote in both languages: the little song "In the Bay" from time of his first setting foot in the country.

In the beginning of *Journey and Experience,* superscribed *On the Origin of My Own Poems,* the poet has very soberly described how the Hebrew, and later the German, version arose. For a direct comparison we are only given here an indication for the beginning and the conclusion. In the German poem it runs, "You lay sand / Pure as fire . . ." But in the Hebrew it had read, "You laid sand / Burning purity . . ." Here there is no "as" but the single image, formed out of two words, which were not an adjective and a noun, however, but a participle and a noun. The expression of the vision had assumed a dynamic character. Still more: the Hebrew word that means purity works with full concreteness; the German word cannot be fully divested of its abstractness. But the adjective together with the noun of the elements that are compared says from the other, the German side, what is to be said, the same and yet no longer the same. Otherwise, but no less distinctively, are the two final verses of the one version and the other related to each other. In German they read, "And my senses like ears of grain / Fall." In Hebrew it had run, "And my senses fall like ears of grain, / Waste away." In this concluding word that in German would have destroyed the form of the poem, the primal Hebraic, the biblical inclination to an expansive completeness transmits itself. And one final remark. In the middle of the poem, at the beginning of the second stanza, we read in the German version, "Nothing other than / Beholding do I want . . ." In the Hebrew version in contrast the first verse of this stanza (which stands for the two German ones) says, "And to my soul I spoke: Awake, behold!" Here the central might of the biblical soul, the dialogical, has overpowered the poet. In the transition to the German form he had to free himself from it.

Our age has recognized more clearly than those before us that the genuineness of the true poem shows itself in the completed unity of content and form. To the few who have recognized this so clearly belongs Ludwig Strauss. This insight of ours helps us to understand that "pair of lips" as a pair of souls, in the framework of a great process of the history of the spirit.

SINCE WE HAVE BEEN A DIALOGUE

To the Memory of Ludwig Strauss

"Seit ein gesprach wir sind / Und horen können voninander" [Since we have been a dialogue / And can
each hear the other"] (the conclusion of the poem "Versöhnender der du nimmer geglaubt" ["Reconciler, you, never
believed"] in the third version).

Hölderlin does not say, "Since we have been in dialogue";
he says and means, "Since we have been *a* dialogue."

The explanation "Since the gods have led us into dialogue"
(Heidegger) does not do justice to what is said. We ourselves
are the dialogue: we are spoken (cf. the beginning of the
second version of "Mnemosyne": "Ein Zeichen sind wir,
deutungslos." ["We are a sign, uninterpreted."])

Our being spoken is our existence. Just thereby it is also
"divine gift" ("Versöhnender," first and second versions),
indeed it is the real gift. But speech only fulfills itself when
it has become "possession" through us ourselves (second
version) and we may now call "the human divine" (*ibid.*)
ours.

In the measure that each of us reveals himself to the others,
fulfilling the speech that he is, we allow the Coming One to
come until out of the ability to hear that characterizes existence in reciprocity, "all experience one another" and so in
the renewed "silence" in the "evening of time" there is again
"a speech among the living" and the pure voices resound together, no longer a dialogue but "a chorus now" (unfinished
conclusion*), the dead with the living, hence "all mortals

---

* I follow in this point Hellingrath (instead of Beissner).

whom we know until now," "all one in you" (*ibid.*), in "the God of gods" (first version), who uttered and heard them have dialogue with the gods, the messengers to whom he is God.

Additional Comment

This indication of the meaning of a verse of Hölderlin's I set down in October 1952 for a presentation composed of the handwritten utterances of friends for the sixtieth birthday of Ludwig Strauss (d. 1953). The "Friedensfeier" ("Peace celebration") that has become known since then has altered nothing in my view. The new version "but soon we are song" shows, however, how in the poet the ontic vision to which I pointed has become clear. To be "a choir" means to bring forth song together; but now Hölderlin promises men that out of their being as dialogue will come a being as song. To the dialogue indeed belongs the persevering in the tension during the nearing; in song all tensions are melted down. Only when those whose dialogue we are sing us are we We.

COMMENTS ON
THE IDEA OF COMMUNITY

THE AMBIGUITY of the concept that is employed is greater here than anywhere else. One says, for example, that socialism is the passing of the control over the means of production from the hands of the entrepreneur into that of the collective; but everything depends on what one understands by collective. If it is what we are accustomed to call the state, *i.e.,* an institution in which an essentially unstructured mass lets its business be conducted by a so-called representation, then in a socialist society essentially this will have changed, that the workers will feel themselves to be represented by the possessors of the power of the disposal of the means of production. But what is representation? Is it not in the all too far-reaching allowing-oneself-to-be-represented that the worst defect of modern society lies? And in a socialist society will not the economic letting-oneself-be-represented be added to the political so that only then for the first time the almost unlimited being-represented and thereby the almost unlimited central accumulation of power will predominate? But the more a human group lets itself be represented in the determination of its common affairs and the more from outside, so much the less community life exists in it, so much the poorer in community does it become. For community— not the primitive but that which is possible and suitable for us men of today—proclaims itself above all in the common active handling of the common and cannot endure without it.

The primal hope of all history depends upon a genuine, hence thoroughly *communally disposed* community of the human race. Fictitious, counterfeit, a planet-size lie would be the unity that was not established out of real communal living of smaller and larger groups that dwell or work together and out of their reciprocal relationships. Everything depends therefore upon the collective, into whose hands the control over the means of production will pass, making possible and demanding by its structure and its institutions real communal living of manifold groups, indeed that these groups themselves become the true subjects of the process of production; thus that the mass be as articulated and in its articulations (the various communes) be as powerful as the common economy of mankind affords; thus that the centralistic letting-oneself-be-represented only extend so far as the new order absolutely demands. The inner question of destiny does not take the form of a fundamental Either-Or: it is the question of the legitimating, ever-newly-drawn demarcation line, the thousandfold system of demarcation lines between the realms that it is necessary to centralize and those that it is necessary to liberate, between the law of unity and the claim of community. The unremitting testing of the current state of things from the standpoint of the claim of the community as that which is always liable to oppression by the central power, the vigilance concerning the *truth of the boundary,* ever changing according to the changing historical conditions, would be the task of the spiritual conscience of mankind, a high court of an unheard-of kind, the reliable representation of the living idea. The Platonic "guardians" await here a new form of manifestation.

The representative of the idea, I say, not a rigid principle but the living form [*Gestalt*] that now wants to become malleable to be shaped in the material of just this earth day. Community too may not become principle; it too, when it appears, shall satisfy not a concept but a situation. Realization of the idea of community, like the realization of any idea, does not exist once for all and generally valid but always only as the moment's answer to a moment's question.

For the sake of this, its life meaning, all sentimentality, all exaggeration and overenthusiasm must be kept far from our thinking about community. Community is never mood, and even where it is feeling, it is always the feeling of a *state of existence*. Community is the inner constitution of a common life that knows and embraces the parsimonious "account," the opposing "accident," the suddenly invading "care." It is commonness of need and only from this commonness of spirit, commonness of trouble and only from this commonness of salvation. Even that community that calls the spirit its master and salvation its promise, the "religious," is only community when it serves its master in the unselective, unexalted simple reality that it has not chosen for itself, that rather, just thus, has been sent; only when it prepares the way for its promise through the brambles of this pathless hour. Certainly, "works" are not required, but the work of faith is required. It is only truly a community of faith when it is a community of work.

The real essence of community is undoubtedly to be found in the—manifest or hidden—fact that it has a center. The real origin of community is undoubtedly only to be understood by the fact that its members have a common relationship to the center superior to all other relations: the circle is drawn from the radii, not from the points of the periphery. And undoubtedly the primal reality of the center cannot be known if it is not known as transparent into the divine. But the more earthly, the more creaturely, the more bound a character the circle takes, so much the truer, the more transparent it is. The "social" belongs to it. Not as a subdivision but as the world of authentication: in which the truth of the center proves itself. The early Christians were not satisfied with the communes that were next to or above the world, and they went into the desert so as to have no community except that with God and no more disturbing world. But it was shown to them that God does not will that man be alone with him, and above the holy impotence of solitude grew the brotherly order. Finally, overstepping the realm of Benedict, Francis established the bond with the creatures.

Yet a community does not need to be founded. When historical destiny had put a human band in a common nature- and life-space, there was space for the development of a genuine commune; and no altar of a city god was necessary in the center if the inhabitants knew themselves united for the sake of and through the Unnamable. A living and ever- renewed togetherness was given and needed only to be de- veloped in the immediacy of all relationships. The common concerns were deliberated and decided in common—in the most favorable cases not through representatives but in the gathering in the marketplace, and the unification experienced in public radiated out into each personal contact. The danger of seclusion might threaten: the spirit expelled it, which thrived here as nowhere else and broke its great window into the narrow walls for the sake of a vision of people, humanity, cosmos.

But, objectors tell me, that is now quite irrecoverable. The modern city has no agora, and modern man has no time for the transactions of which he can be relieved by his chosen representatives. A concrete togetherness is already destroyed by the compulsion of quantity and the form of organization. Work joins one to other persons than leisure does, sport to others than politics; day and soul are tidily divided. But the ties are just factual, one pursues together the common in- terests and tendencies and has no use for "immediacy." Col- lectivity is no intimate crouching down together but a great economic or political union of forces, unproductive for ro- mantic play of the imagination but comprehensible as num- bers, expressing itself in actions and effects to which the individual may belong without intimacies but in consciousness of his energetic contribution. Those "bonds" that resist the inevitable development must dissolve. There is still the family, to be sure, which as a house-community appears to demand and to guarantee a measure of living life together, but it too will emerge out of the crisis into which it has entered as a union for a purpose, or it will disappear.

In opposition to this mixture of correct evidence and distorted conclusions, I espouse the rebirth of the commune. Rebirth, not restoration. It cannot be restored in fact, although it seems to me that each breath of neighborliness in the apartment building, each wave of a warmer comradeship during the rest period in the highly rationalized factory means a growth of communal-mindedness of the world, and although at times an upright village commune pleases me more than a parliament. It cannot be restored. But whether a rebirth of the commune takes place out of the waters and the spirit of the approaching transformation of society—by this, it seems to me, the lot of the human species will be determined. An organic communal being—and only such is suitable for a formed and articulated mankind—will never be erected out of individuals, only out of small and the smallest communities: a people is community to the extent that it is communally disposed.

If the family does not emerge from the crisis, which today appears like ruin, purified and renewed, then the form of statehood will end up by being only a furnace which will be fueled with the bodies of the generations. The commune which can be renewed in such a manner exists only as a residue. If I speak of a rebirth, I do not think of a continuing, but of a changed world situation. By the new communes— one could also call them the new fellowships—I mean the subject of the transformed economy, the collective into whose hands the control over the means of production shall pass. Once again: everything depends upon whether they will be made ready, whether they will be ready.

How much of economic and political autonomy will be accorded them—for they will necessarily be economic and political unities at the same time—is a technical question that one has to pose and to answer ever anew, but to pose and to answer from the standpoint of the more than technical knowledge that the inner might of a community is also conditional upon its outer strength. The relation of centralism and decentralization is a problem that, as has been said, is to be dealt with not fundamentally but, like everything that concerns the traffic of the idea with reality, with the great tact of the spirit, with the untiring weighing of the legitimate How Much. Centralization, yes, but only so much as must be centralized according to the conditions of the time and the place; if the high court that is summoned to the drawing and new drawing of the line of demarcation remains awake in its conscience, then the division between base and apex of the power pyramid will be entirely different from today's, even in states that call themselves communist, which certainly still means striving for community. A system of representation must also exist in the form of society that I have in mind; but it will not present itself, like those of today, in the seeming representation of amorphous masses of voters but in the work-tested representatives of economic communities. The represented will not be bound with their representatives in empty abstractions, through the phraseology of a party program, as today, but concretely, through common activity and common experience.

But the most essential must be that the process of the formation of community must continue into the relations of the communities to each other. Only a community of communities may be called a communal being.

The picture that I have hastily sketched will be put on the shelf of "utopian socialism" until the storm turns over the leaves again. Just as I do not believe in Marx's "gestation" of the new form of society, so I do not believe in Bakunin's virgin birth out of the womb of the revolution. But I believe in the meeting of image and destiny in the plastic hour.

COMMUNITY AND ENVIRONMENT

IF ONE SEEKS to transport the great social question from its sublime dialectical abstractness into the concrete language of the reality in which we live, it turns out that the various formulations of this question without exception have an essentially quantitative character; for example, "What is, with the greatest possible productivity of the total economy, the maximum share of the working man in the fruits of his labor, and what measures shall be taken in order to let him have this maximum?" Through the intellectual and material power which this kind of question and its consequences have assumed in our age, a series of fully concrete "little" questions have been pushed aside or suppressed, questions of an eminently qualitative character, such as, "How does the worker work at present in a factory highly developed in the techniques of work? As a man or as an external part of a machine? And how in the future can technique be set the task of including man as man in its calculations?" For him who is concerned that man live in the whole context of his existence as man, these "little" questions—which will continue to exist however those others are solved—are great ones, and he is concerned, each in his own sphere, to point out the direction and to guard it.

One such question goes: "How are the men of the modern civilization housed and how must they be housed in order to live as men?" There is no more concrete and current question.

I remember having read more than forty years ago in a book of Chesterton's (not word for word but approximately) that the solution of the social question is to be found in each

93

94 A BELIEVING HUMANISM

having a house of his own. These days I read in the newspaper that the prime minister of Burma has promised his people a welfare state in which each citizen shall have his own house. This sort of statement rings in our ears like a romantic utopia, hence like a utopia which lacks the most precious quality of a utopia: to be unromantic. But it is not so romantic and also not so utopian as it sounds; for it is bound up with one of those primal demands of the human heart which at any moment, overnight, will break through to actualization and become self-evident. Man not only *must* have a dwelling, he also *wants* it. And he wants to dwell in a house. But in the imperishable primal language of the human heart house means my house, your house, a man's own house. The house is the winning throw of the dice* which man has wrested from the uncanniness of universe; it is his defense against the chaos that threatens to invade him. Therefore his deeper wish is that it be his own house, that he not have to share with anyone other than his own family.

All this, nonetheless, is still only the presupposition for what is most important, when we finally attain to the knowledge that the essential human reality is no longer to be regarded as one of the individual life (even as little as one of the collective life), but as something that takes place between man and man, between I and Thou. For the house of man about which he is concerned no longer stands just anywhere, no matter where, in a splendid isolation for example, as long as he can easily get from there to his place of work, where he must perhaps for so and so many hours share a space with "strange" men, in order then quickly and completely to leave them and to go home [*nach Hause*]. Rather the house of man about which he is concerned now stands

---

* The German original—*der feste Würfel*—contains a pun. The word for dice also means cube, while *feste* means both winning throw and firm. Hence "winning throw of the dice" equals "a firm cube" equals "a house"—M.F.

between houses, between neighboring houses, between the houses of his neighbors.

The unavowed secret of man is that he wants to be confirmed in his being and his existence by his fellow men and that he wishes them to make it possible for him to confirm them, and, to be sure, the former and the latter not merely in the family, in the party assembly or in the public house, but also in the course of neighborly encounters, perhaps when he or the other steps out of the door of his house or to the window of his house and the greeting with which they greet each other will be accompanied by a glance of well-wishing, a glance in which curiosity, mistrust, and routine will have been overcome by a mutual sympathy: the one gives the other to understand that he affirms his presence. This is the indispensable minimum of humanity. If the world of man is to become a human world, then immediacy must rule between men, and thus also between human house and human house. And as in everything else, so also here the institutional and the educational influence must supplement each other. The secret longing of man for a life in reciprocal mutual confirmation must be developed through education, but the external conditions it needs in order to find its fulfillment must also be created. The architects must be set the task of also building for human contact, building surroundings that invite meeting and centers that shape meeting.

This book wishes to serve the rebirth of the human dialogue from the standpoint of architecture. Therein lies its importance.

THE THIRD LEG OF THE TABLE

WHEN Rabbi Yeheskel Landau came to Prague, he spoke to his congregation Sabbath after Sabbath of nothing else except the bitter need of the destitute in the city. One had expected to hear from his mouth profound meanings of interpretations and subtle meanings of disputations, but he only thought of reminding them of the wretched who spread out unrelieved, unnoticed, in this lane and its surroundings. "Help! Go there even today in the evening and help!" thus he called ever again. But the people took it for a sermon and were vexed that it was so insipid and flat.

Then on a busy market day something wonderful took place. Right through the middle of the tumult came the rabbi and remained standing in the center of the thickest swarm as though he had wares to offer for sale and only waited for a favorable moment to commend them to the crowd. Those who recognized him passed the incomprehensible fact on to others; from everywhere traders and buyers crowded to that place; they stared at him, but no one dared to question him. Finally there broke from the lips of one who imagined himself intimate with him, "What is our rabbi doing here?"

At once Rabbi Yeheskel began:

"If a table has three legs and a piece is broken off of one of the three legs, what does one do? One supports the leg as well as one can, and the table stands. But now if still another of the three legs breaks in two, there is no longer a support. What does one do then? One shortens the third leg too, and the table stands again.

"Our sages say: 'The world stands on three things: on the

teaching, on the service, and on the deeds of love.' When the holiness is destroyed, then the leg of the service breaks. Then our sages support it by saying: 'Service with the heart, that is what is meant by prayer.' But now when the acts of love disappear and the second leg suffers injury, how shall the world still endure? Therefore, I have left the house of teaching and have come to the market place. We must shorten the leg of the teaching in order that the table of the world may again stand firm."

EDUCATING

       I AM inclined, within the concept of education, to hold the significance of drawing forth to be the decisive one. After that—in contrast to the so beloved perceptible and imperceptible imposition of the preconceived view and attitude of a party and the like, which one may perhaps describe as propaganda—it is a question of fetching forth out of the child or youth something latent and cultivating it. But what is it that one should fetch forth? It is usual to answer such a question with a pair of general ethical categories. They are not sufficient. It is an inadmissible simplification to assume that in all children the same general treasure is hidden. Despite all common traits, we are ultimately without exception *unica,* and the treasure that is hidden in each child is something irreducibly personal. However cruelly injuries of all kinds affect the child from his mother's womb to school and beyond it, the primal fact of the positive determination of the person is to me certain. One misses and misses it, but it is never wanting. But what is it then which is meant here by educating—by drawing out and drawing upward? No content of an utterance, but the speaking voice; no instructing, but the glance, the movement, the being-there of those teaching when they are inspired by the educational task. Relationship educates [*Beziehung erzieht*], provided that it is a genuine educational relationship.

THE TASK

ACCORDING TO the dominating concept of edution, it is the transmission of the values of one generation to a following, in such a manner that this latter not only accept them but acknowledge them as its own, suitable to it and to be exhibited by it anew. This concept prevails, in many kinds of disguises, in the institutions shaped by the present societies and their organs.

It goes back to a basic relation of man to man which one can designate as the political. In it one sees the other beings around one as centers of productivity which need to be recognized and employed in their specific capacities, as bundles of experienceable, influenceable, manageable, usable properties. Each one is to him a He or a She, constituted thus and thus, bearing in himself such and such possibilities of which those are to be furthered in their unfolding that can be made useful for the utilitarian goal. From this basic relation the public life of the present, within the peoples and between the peoples, has sprung up; it extends far into personal life, only now and then interrupted by cursory vistas of love, friendship, comradeship, fleeting revelations of the Thou, after which man, as if nothing had happened, resumes at any given time the usual practice. Applied to the relation of the grown-up to the child and to the youth, it yields what today in general is called education.

In opposition to this primal evil of modern man, which is already preparing to annihilate him and his world, there arises in this hour of pain, of question, of rebellion, before the genuine bearers of these three, before those pained in their world conscience, before those who question out of their world faith, who rebel with their world love, the word of exorcism and of healing: not your It, your Thou is what is essential, though not surveyable. It is infinite in its possibilities, which nonetheless remain peculiar to it, possibilities given to you not for utilization but for opening up and redemption, all of them to each of you; if you make use of them, you will ruin them and yourself. Education arises, no longer subservient to the political relation, willing to melt down and to transform the political human realm, decisive without haste, ready to serve without fanaticism, prepared to wait and yet beginning—and reflecting on the mystery of how the starry sky, the forest, and everything unarbitrary educates in incomprehensible moments, the man already stands in his new work.

Education is opening up. But already it begins to become manifest that this signifies more than letting the youthful being develop out of itself and watching over its development. For in our meeting, even when we no more want to intervene than the heavens and the forest, there is something powerfully stirring—our saying of Thou. Here begins our secret might and its responsibility. Man exercises power even in the most involuntary: everything depends upon whether he knows what he does and places it under the law of his task. Ah, what is your love if it is not also responsibility for everything that is effected by its might! Whether we intend it or not, we always educate "to" something; it depends upon us whether that something is what we do not will or something that we do will—will without willfulness. But this can only be done legitimately in one way, which is what we ourselves do in educating, since we live facing man as our Thou, not experiencing him but beholding him, not using but realizing. That he lives thus, facing the beings in their true presence and truly present to them, saying Thou to them, awakening the Thou in them, familiar with the All, with the All intimate, that our union with it may effect in it All unity. It is that which we will when we, educating without willfulness, will. Only he can educate who stands in the eternal presence; he educates by leading them into it. Religious education as a partial sphere must become more and more problematic; but education is only a whole when it is religious as a whole. That principle becomes visibly manifest that sets its face against that of annihilation. Only when man is melted down and transformed will this become the human realm.

ON CONTACT

CAN ONE educate through instruction? Instruction wants to influence the thinking of the pupil, education his being and life. Is it sufficient, as Socrates believed, to awaken the knowledge of the right in him for the right to be realized in his being and life? But even Socrates himself exercised his decisive effect not through what he taught but through his life. It is not the instruction that educates but the instructor. The good teacher educates by his speech and by his silence, in the hours of teaching and in the recesses, in casual conversation, through his mere existence, only he must be a really existing man and he must be really present to his pupils; he educates through contact.

Contact is the primary word of education. It means that the teacher shall face his pupils not as developed brain before unfinished ones, but as being before beings, as mature being before developing beings. He must really face them, that means not in a direction working from above to below, from the teacher's chair to the pupils' benches, but in genuine interaction, in exchange of experiences, experiences of a fulfilled life with those of still unfulfilled ones. But the latter experiences are no less important than the former. For what is needed is not mere seeking for information from below and giving information from above, also not mere questions from here and answers from there, but genuine dialogue. The teacher, to be sure, conducts and governs this dialogue, but even so he must also enter it with his own person, directly and candidly. This dialogue shall continue into silent being with one another, indeed undoubtedly only here will it first properly culminate. It is this which I call the dialogical principle in education.

STYLE AND INSTRUCTION

OF THE two modes of written expression, different in essence and in style—communication and literature —the school has only to nourish, stimulate, and cultivate the first, the basic types of which are the letter and the diary (which in no way means that one should assign compositions in the form of letters and diaries). In the face of the sphere of literary expression, it must educate in the student understanding for its special and separate nature, that is, respect for charisma.

The old composition rests upon the spirit-forsaken fiction that one can "give back" the "content" of a work "in other words"; it confounds the law of communication, according to which, in fact, a what can be expressed in this or that manner, with the law of creation that knows no What hiding behind a How, no coming together and coming apart of material and form, but only the indivisible unity of the corporeal idea. It thereby contributes to killing in young men the glimpse of the spiritual world, in which the one thing needed rules and no word can take the place of another, and it allows to grow to a power of perversion the lawless swarm, the unholy band of dwellers in a spectral realm between the objective and subjective world, the writers who "can write," rather than "*must* write."

The new composition shall have for its presupposition the knowledge of the boundary and the duty of guarding its purity. Like all the instruments of a legitimate, more-unfolding-than-imposing instruction, it shall not proceed from an arbitrary setting of an aim but from a natural spontaneity of the young man: it shall tie itself to his need to communicate (the school does not need to be concerned about those quite rare cases where this is the forerunner of the creative urge); and, to be sure, to the various needs of communication of the different age levels.

When one tests these comparatively, one will probably be able to distinguish three stages. The first may be essentially the communication of intentions, the second of perception, the third of thoughts. I might have the real writing of essays begin no earlier than with the fourteenth or still better the fifteenth year. Before then there should only be exercises in composing short, brief, "naked" sentences, without accessories, exercises in the clearest formulation of all kinds of things spoken about in school, hence only in the midst of instruction and as occasional additions to the oral (whereby ideally the right thing would be to distribute these exercises among all the subjects of instruction). With the completion of the fourteenth or the fifteenth year, *i.e.,* with the beginning differentiation of the need to communicate, one could pass on to the "assigned" essay, of course with far-reaching freedom in the choice of theme by the pupil within the general directive.

In the first, shortest stage the pupils would have for their projects many kinds of things to tell (that the desire and honesty of the communication in them must be developed through the right personal relationship of the teacher, through the awakening of a deep trust, I surely need not emphasize); in the second, longest stage they would have to note down what they have seen and heard and, of course, first of all objects (competent description of a limited next-to-one-another), later occurrences (competent report of a limited after-one-another); in the third stage, which would perhaps be that of the highest school class, the communication of a thought completely enclosed in itself in clear, precise, and simple form should always be sought (a thought concerning a common theme, yet the thoughts must rise in the pupils themselves and are also—perhaps not before the writing down but probably on the strength of the adequacy of the style, *after* it—to be discussed in common). As a general basic principle for all stages it would be valid to say, "Write only what you want to communicate; write so that it is communicated."

AN EXAMPLE:
ON THE LANDSCAPES
OF LEOPOLD KRAKAUER

LEOPOLD KRAKAUER, who lived in Jerusalem and some years ago died there, belonged to no school and emulated no style, neither a new nor an old; his own vision inspired in him his own language. He was a solitary man; but his solitude was a speaking, a formative one, indeed, one may say that it was his solitude that brought him to his work. That happened on the path of a meeting which became Krakauer's artistic destiny: that with the landscape of Jerusalem. His solitude met that of the landscape and transformed itself in it. Only in drawing the Jerusalemite solitude did he become the artist that he was.

Krakauer carried nothing "from above" into nature. He entered into the very phenomenon that accosted him, but he did it with so powerful a devotion that he was able to grasp it from its inwardness, as it were, in the dynamic of its solitude that corresponded to and answered his own. The inner tension that works out of the restless and yet so finished form of the thistle, the great inner trembling that is frozen into the limbs of the olive tree as the life pain of a man into the lines of his face, yes even the immeasurable movement of the smallest little part that hides behind the apparent deadness of a heap of stones but that lets something like a strange knocking penetrate from itself to us—all that is intensified in Krakauer's pages to the language of a solitude, a solitary torment at the very base of each creature. It is intensified, I say, but this intensification works on us like a discovery. That at times in a drawing of Krakauer's such a tree almost appears to us like a human shape means nothing fantastic; it belongs to the essence of this peculiar vision of nature.

Under the impression of some of his drawings of olive trees, I once told Krakauer to his surprise of the West Manichaean conception of Jesus *patibilis,* a cosmic or rather tellurian Christ figure which, imprisoned in the plants of nature, suffers its forsakenness hanging in every tree. Such a mythical image had never been present to Leopold Krakauer's mind; he was never concerned with anything save as marks on a piece of paper to make visible the vision that encountered the artist in his personal meetings with nature. Before one of his olive-tree drawings, Krakauer could ask, "Does one see the turning into wood?" Or also, "Does one see the grasping of the roots into the earth?" Yes, one saw this, one saw that; but he had *suffered* both—in his vision which was a suffering.

Emil Preetorius has often raised the question, and most recently with an especial insistence, whether today nature still confronts us, whether for the artist in this our changed world the how must not step into the place of the what, or, in Preetorius' own words, whether it is not now the medium of the picture itself which becomes the reality facing us, a facing, of course, which is located in the inwardness of the artist. But here there is no distinction made, which I hold to be indispensable, between face-to-face being and passive object [*Gegenüber und Gegenstand*]. With objects there is no dialogue (Preetorius also employs this concept); it exists only with face-to-face being; but in the inwardness of man there exists no real face-to-face and accordingly no real dialogue. What is more, the how is not something that first appears in becoming a work; already in the meeting itself it is there, for it is not the perception of an object that furnishes us with a what but the being accosted by face-to-face being that enables the human person to behold superobjectively. Even the animal has objects, only man has face-to-face being, and he has it just as man.

Certainly, in the forlornness of today it may at times appear as though we had been deprived of the meeting with nature; in truth, however, we do not stand in a changed but in a changing world; and this changing is a process that does not take place independently of our willing and our repugnance. Preetorius says rightly that a question such as that discussed by him cannot be answered theoretically but only through the deed. But must we regard the renunciation of the personal contact with nature as the essential deed of the coming generation of artists? "Turning away from appearance," Preetorius calls it, but in the genuine meetings with a Thou it is never appearance but always the completed presence that has ruled. A familiar or an overpoweringly unfamiliar being that approaches us is not to be identified with any "impression of the eyes." Our senses are not sufficient by far to withstand what moves toward us. Nature too moves toward us, even in the most extreme motionlessness; it has to do with us.

It is my judgment that tomorrow, in the crisis of all crises, the deed of the coming generation of artists can and may be to seek a breakthrough to a new, transformed meeting with nature. Already today we notice in many places the hidden or manifest longing for it. The work of Leopold Krakauer gives unmistakable testimony to it.

RELIGION AND GOD'S RULE

To THE BOOK *Weltreich, Religion und Gottes-herrschaft* [*The Kingdom of the World, Religion, and God's Rule*] by Leonhard Ragaz,* the work of a man who in the earnestness of personal life has penetrated through the labyrinthine mirrorings of theology to the reality of God and the word, I might draw attention first of all because here on the part of a Christian, but essentially valid for the religious man everywhere, a distinction is drawn with all the sharpness one might wish between religion and the kingdom of God. Ragaz sees in the kingdom of God "rather the opposite of religion." He knows that Moses, the prophets, and Jesus do not mean a religion but a kingdom, a condition of the world in accord with God. He finds "in religion no guarantee that in it we have to do with God himself. One can have a great deal of religion and be far from God, indeed godless," for "religion has the tendency to become a thing that is important for its own sake," it reaches the point of "putting itself in the place of God, hiding the absence of His kingdom through religion." Statements like these deserve an emphatic praise at all times for their healthy decisiveness. Today a special merit pertains

---

* Two volumes. Erlenbach-Zurich: Rotapfel-Verlag. In the same publishing house in the collection *Flugschriften der Quelle* appeared the excellent Blumhardt book of Ragaz, *Der Kampf um das Reich Gottes* ("The Struggle for the Kingdom of God"), as well as the supplementary pamphlets, *"Die Erlösung durch die Liebe,"* ("Redemption through Love"), *"Selbstbehauptung und Selbstverleugnung"* (Self-Affirmation and Self-Denial"), *Theosophie oder Reich Gottes?"* ("Theosophy or the Kingdom of God?"), and *"Judentum und Christentum"* ("Judaism and Christianity").

to them because they say what is right in the very midst of the thickest perversity.

The largest part of what is today called religion is perverted—not perhaps in the individual details of its contents, but in its whole structure. One wills something there that one need only just will in order to miss it. It is indeed characteristic of the "movements" of this age that they strive for usual things that can only arise as byproducts—thus at first "personality" was striven for, which perhaps arises when a man has his work in mind with the might of his being; after that "community," which perhaps arises when some men have an action in mind in just such a way that they can only accomplish it in common. Thus one now strives also for "religion," which, in so far as it is in general something real, arises there where men have God in mind with the might of their being. If, on the contrary, they have religion in mind instead, what sorts of malformations must come together there!

But the religious movement is in a worse plight than the others. Work and personality, common action and community can indeed, after the byproduct has once been engendered, exist quite well beside each other and be conducive to each other. But as often as religion has appeared once again in history, there was also in it a force that—not in a doubtful manner like the profane forces, but with the appearance of the highest legitimacy—diverted man from God. That it thereby enjoyed a great success was caused for the most part by the fact that it is far more comfortable to have to do with religion than to have to do with God, who sends one out of home and fatherland into restless wandering. In addition, religion has all kinds of aesthetic refreshments to offer its cultivated adherents (whereby it has also then frequently become a division of the aesthetic), whereas God transforms for man even formation and vision in a sacrifice that is offered, to be sure, by a joyful but not by an enjoying heart. For this reason, at all times the awake spirits have been vigilant and have warned of the diverting force hidden in religion—which is, indeed, only the highest sublimation of the force that manifests itself in all life spheres in their cruder autonomization, in their tearing loose from the whole life and in the attempt, instead of subsuming conditionally autonomous multiplicity under the one world law, to allow a unity-blind being-a-law-unto-itself to dominate.

This warning has hardly, however, been so needed as today when the one world has broken asunder for man into a multiplicity of independent and unconnected spheres each of which pretends to embrace the whole in a "spiritual form." Between them not even a war of all against all rages, since none fundamentally claims to be reality; all rather are meant as levels on which the creative subjectivity bustles about. Such a level is the largest part of what in the present religious movement is called religion. There exists, we are told, a religious relation to the world, as an aesthetic or a philosophical one exists; there exist series of religious experiences as there exist series of erotic and of political experiences; one is simply not wholly in order if one does not possess these highest and most select of experiences; and this relation, this series of experiences, gets along splendidly with those others in the well-assorted camp of modern subjectivism. But either religion is a reality, rather *the* reality, namely the *whole* existence of the real man in the real world of God, an existence that unites all that is partial; or it is a phantom of the covetous human soul, and then it would be right promptly and completely to replace its rituals by art, its commands by ethics, its revelations by science.

In opposition to the usual way of getting a perspective on God and the world, the warning of a man like Ragaz comes at the right time. But he must also be affirmed in another, still more important, respect that can only be touched on here. Ragaz poses the question of questions, that concerning the *kingdom,* and he does it in a time that is eschatologically moved—in Eastern Europe by eschatological impulses, in Central Europe by eschatological thoughts, in Western Europe at least by eschatological moods. He makes the clear, simple demand that the kingdom of God, although its innermost truth does not have its dwelling in time, must be regarded by man in his reality which comes in time; although that time may be other than the one in which we live, a way leads from this time to that; and, even though we injure ourselves by every will to produce it, we have a share in its becoming the limits of which only the deed can measure.

FRAGMENTS ON REVELATION

The Place of Reason in Revelation

Revelation is continual, and everything is fit to become a sign of revelation. What is disclosed to us in the revelation is not God's essence as it is independent of our existence, but his relationship to us and our relationship to him. We can only receive revelation, if when and so long as we are a whole. In this wholeness, in which all my forces and capacities are included, reason, of course, cannot be lacking; it too must enter into the oneness as which alone I can receive revelation. But in order to do this, it must abandon the claim to exist for itself and to be sufficient unto itself. If reason has fit itself in as one of the elements in the wholeness of our substance, then it cannot happen that what is experienced in revelation contradicts it although it may contradict its earlier insights. The reason that has entered into the whole is ready to allow its earlier conclusions to be overturned or at least corrected. Revelation thereby summons reason to take part in its reception but also to allow itself to be stirred and renewed by it.

On the Nature of Authority in Religion

Genuine authority exists in religion as in general in the world only in so far as God's will is known. But a full and adequate knowledge of God's will does not exist in history. In the moment when it should enter history, history would be at an end. The factual event of revelation in history, even as in the lives of individual men, does not mean that a divine

content pours into an empty human vessel or that a divine
substance presents itself in human form. The factual revelation means the breaking of the united light of God into human multiplicity, that is, the breaking of the unity into
contradiction. We know no other revelation than that of the
meeting of the divine and the human in which the human has
a factual share. The divine is a fire that melts again the
human ore, but what is produced is not of the nature of the
fire. We cannot, therefore, understand what directly or indi-
rectly (be it through written or oral tradition) proceeds from
the factual revelation, whether word or custom or institution
as we possess it, as spoken by God or established by God. But
it is also not given to us simply and once for all to distinguish between the divine and the human within it. In other
words: there is no security against the necessity of living in
fear and trembling; there is nothing else than the certainty
that we share in the revelation. Nothing can relieve us of the
task of opening ourselves as we are, as a whole and a unity,
to the continual revelation that can make all, all things and
all events, in history and in our lives, into its signs. Only thus
can we win the foundation for an at once faithful and critical
attitude. We win the foundation on our own responsibility,
hence with fear and trembling, which enables us to distinguish within each genuine authority, *i.e.,* one whose origin
out of real meeting of the divine and the human is certain to
us in faith, between these two for this one definite particular
hour, and, of course, not simply that but only in the realm of
our own decisions—hence only by distinguishing within ourselves. World history is the battleground between false and
genuine authority; each man of faith is obliged to take part in
this battle and to contribute to the victory of the genuine
authority; the victories that are gained here are for the most
part underground and only later become recognizable. But
world history is also the plunge bath in which each genuine
authority must ever again purify itself, seek to free itself from
the slag of the human which has become perceptible as such;

each man of faith is obliged to take part in it through self refining. Here too the event often announces itself only in future epochs.

The Exclusive Attitude of the Religions

Every religion has its origin in a revelation. No religion is absolute truth, none is a piece of heaven that has come down to earth. Each religion is a human truth. That means it represents the relationship of a particular human community as such to the Absolute. Each religion is a house of the human soul longing for God, a house with windows and without a door; I need only open a window and God's light penetrates; but if I make a hole in the wall and break out, then I have not only become houseless but a cold light surrounds me that is not the light of the living God. Each religion is an exile into which man is driven; here he is in exile more clearly than elsewhere because in his relationship to God he is separated from the men of other communities; and not sooner than in the redemption of the world can we be liberated from the exiles and brought into the common world of God. But the religions that know that are bound together in common expectation; they can call to one another greetings from exile to exile, from house to house through the open windows. Yet not that alone: they can enter into association with one another and seek to clarify with one another what can be done from the side of mankind to bring redemption nearer. A common action of religions is conceivable even though each of them cannot act elsewhere than in its own house. But all that is only possible to the extent to which each religion turns to its origin, to the revelation in which it has its origin, and practices criticism of the withdrawal from it that has taken place in its historical process of development. The historical religions have the tendency to become ends in themselves and, as it were, to put themselves in God's place, and, in fact, there is nothing that is so apt to obscure the face of God as a religion. The religions must become submissive to God and his will; each must recognize that it is only one of the shapes in which the human elaboration of the divine message is presented, that it has no monopoly on God; each must renounce being God's house on earth and content itself with being a house of the men who are turned toward the same purpose of God, a house with windows; each must give up its false exclusive attitude and accept the true one. And something more is needed: the religions must hearken with all their force to what God's will for this hour is, they must seek from the standpoint of revelation to overcome the current problems which the contradiction between the will of God and the present reality of the world place before them. Then they will be united not only in the common expectation of redemption but also in the concern for the still unredeemed world.

BELIEVING HUMANISM

THE THANKS of my heart that I want to express in this hour to His Royal Highness Prince Bernhard and the members of the Prize Committee are no thanks of a general sort for a high honor that has fallen to my share: they are entirely special thanks for this particular prize which is bound up with the name of Erasmus. For if I should characterize my own basic view by a concept, it can only be the same as that with which we characterize Erasmus: the concept of a believing humanism.

Yet a distinction is here indispensable, and it is an essential distinction.

The believing humanism of Erasmus signified the uniting of two principles which in the life of man rule next to each other without coming into contact with each other: the natural humanity in which man is at home and which he need only unfold, cultivate, and faith, in which, detaching himself from the human as it were, he raises himself toward God. For this humanism these are two separate spheres in the life of the human person, neither of which limits the other; to each of the two belong special times, special spheres of life.

The view that in our time may be characterized as a believing humanism and that I myself avow is constituted otherwise. Here humanity and faith do not appear as two separate realms each of which stands under its own signs and under its special laws: they penetrate each other, they work together, indeed, they are so centrally related to each other that we may say our faith has our humanity as its foundation, and our humanity has our faith as its foundation.

117

In order to make this relation clearer it is desirable to keep in mind a not unimportant difference between the thinking of the High Renaissance, to which Erasmus is to be ascribed, and the thinking of our own age. It is a question here of the various ways of regarding the *humanum,* what is peculiar to man, what sets him apart distinctively from all the rest of nature, the *humanum* in the most positive sense, that it is incumbent upon us to recognize, to honor, and to cultivate.

In the age of the Renaissance, as already in antiquity, an attempt was often made, to be sure, to define that "human" in the highest sense; but neither in the former case nor in the latter was it indicated with sufficient exactness. Only in our age has human thought determined to know the essence of the *humanum* with the utmost clarity and exactness possible to it, to man. So far as I can see, two essentially different basic answers have been given to the modern question of man concerning himself—and from there also concerning the *humanum* distinguished and to be cultivated by him.

The one, represented by a powerful stream of German philosophy from Hegel to Heidegger, sees in man the being in whom Being attains to consciousness of itself. Accordingly, what is held here to be the preeminent function of man, as the decisive *humanum,* is reflexion,* the reflection on oneself through which, so to speak, he ever again accomplishes the reflection of *Being* on itself. It is probably evident: when a man who understands the *humanum* thus is a believing man, then his humanism and his faith cannot penetrate each other; they will be housed next to each other but they will remain two separate spheres. For the reflexion on Being as that at-

---

* Buber uses "reflexion" here in the physiological sense of bending back on oneself. Hence it is not to be confused with "reflection." See Martin Buber, *Between Man and Man,* trans. by Ronald Gregor Smith with an Introductory Essay by Maurice Friedman (New York: Macmillan Paperbacks, 1965), pp. 22-24. Only here Buber uses in the original German the very term with which Smith rendered *Rückbiegung* into English in *Between Man and Man!*—M.F.

taining self-consciousness in man means just formalized Being, and this radically abstracted from all content. This empty Being, to be sure, is the basic concept of all metaphysics, but in the lived life of the human person, in the life lived by each of us between birth and death, it is not to be met with. Faith, in contrast, means God, and God is present to the human person in the very same lived moment in which he believes in him, or, expressed more truly, trusts in him. He is present, I say, and by that it is not said, "God *is*"—that would transpose him from life into metaphysics; rather by that it is said, "God is *there*." Thus the two spheres do not exist in the life of the modern man of the kind of which I speak, as in the life of the Erasmian man, peacefully next to each other: in the ground of his being he knows that in reality they exclude each other. A genuine believing humanism can no longer grow from this soil.

It is entirely otherwise where, to the question of man concerning himself and concerning the *humanum* that sets him apart from all other earthly creatures and distinguishes him before them, an essentially different answer is given.

In this second answer what is central is not the relation of the human person to himself, not, therefore, that in his own reflexion he uncovers Being that has attained to self-consciousness. What is central, rather, is the relation of man to all existing beings. What appears here as the *humanum,* as the great superiority of man before all other living beings known to us, is his capacity "of his own accord," hence not like the animals out of the compulsion of his needs and wants but out of the overflow of his existence, to come into direct contact with everything that he bodily or spiritually meets— to address it with lips and heart or even with the heart alone. In distinction from the animal, man can grasp all that encounters him on his life way as a being existing in itself beyond his own interests. He can enter into relationship with this independently existing other. By knowing and acknowledging the other at times as a whole, he can at times himself relate to it as a whole. As a whole he enters into the common situations without being consumed in them; for from each he perceives the removed, the special existence not included in this situation, without it thereby becoming for him a mere object of his observation. This other existent being, however little it may take itself out from the fullness of Being, still extends unmeasurably beyond the meeting—and nonetheless it stands in an undiminished partnership with the human person.

In this new answer of our age to the question concerning the *humanum,* this appears thus as the capacity inborn in man to enter into meeting with other existing beings. But since man is the only creature given to our experience in whom this capacity dwells, then we may certainly say that in the history of the world it is first through man that "meeting" has become possible, as meeting of the one with the other.

It is not something incidental but rather of essential significance that in the history of modern philosophy it was either religious thinkers who were inclined to this view, thus in the second half of the eighteenth century Jacobi, in the first half of the nineteenth century Kierkegaard—this latter, of course, limiting the situation of meeting to the relationship between man and God—or thinkers like Kierkegaard's contemporary Feuerbach, who strove to lay the groundwork of a new faith without any transcendent element. As Kierkegaard recognized and acknowledged as essential only the meeting between the individual man and God, so Feuerbach only the meeting between one man and another. Only in our time has the insight into the relationship between I and Thou as an all-embracing one begun to become clear.*

---

* For a much fuller discussion of this development see Buber's Afterword on "The History of the Dialogical Principle," trans. by Maurice Friedman, in *Between Man and Man, loc. cit.,* pp. 209-224—M.F.

Of decisive importance for the problem of an authentic believing humanism in our time, consequently, is the knowledge that the true *humanum* and the experience of faith are rooted in the same soil of meeting. Indeed, the fundamental experience of faith itself may be regarded as the highest intensification of the reality of meeting. That undoubtedly holds for the religious life between the Arabian Sea as the eastern and the Pacific Ocean as the western boundary. But it also appears that far beyond those boundaries, indeed, in the whole human race, a meeting with the ineffable stands at the beginning of the personal experience of faith and also within this it emerges ever again strengthened and renewed.

From this standpoint we can get a glimpse of a modern believing humanism which unites the *humanum* and faith in such a way that they do not merely dwell next to each other but penetrate each other.

Now one might object to my use of the attribute "modern" that precisely in our time very little of such a believing humanism is to be discerned. And, in fact, it will appear that today more than ever a type of man predominates who prefers to observe and make use of the beings whom he encounters on his life way instead of turning soul and deed toward them. But precisely in the present a powerful education toward a new and genuine believing humanism has arisen. I mean the crisis of the human race which threatens it with extinction. I mean the technology that has become leaderless, the unlimited mastery of the means that no longer have to answer to any ends; I mean the voluntary enslavement of man in the service of the split atom. In the growing, the still plastic generation more and more men are aware of what is preparing itself there; their day-by-day-increasing awareness, the knowledge of the crisis, summons in them the only counterforce that can succeed in elevating ends again, great clear ends, above the rebellious means. It is this counterforce that I call the new believing humanism.

From the land of Erasmus I greet the believing humanists in all the world—those who are already active and those who are only ripening.

HOUSE OF GOD

A "BUILDING for worship"—that is surely a space in which a group of men united turns to the divine presence in order to meet it as a unity.

This simple essential turning "thither" has today, in my observation, become something rare and lone. A liturgical or a sacramental occurrence with its techtonic place—ark, altar —can represent and thus make a home for that There; when it displaces it, it obstructs it. How then can a genuine space arise around the seemingly transformed place? How can a legitimate common adjustment of the parts of the building arise when it has no common adjustment of the commune to express and to receive?

Every decent factory building convinces me of the *authenticity of the task:* it is evident that this giver of the task really exists with reliable needs and thereby with reliable incentives for accomplishment. But what is the "religious need" of today for the most part other than a need for religion?

CHASSIDUT

—Ist Chassidut wohl Frömmigkeit zu nennen?
—Irdische Züge lernt ich an ihr kennen.

—So heisst sie Güte dann und Mildigkeit?
—Da bandst du allzusehr sie in die Zeit.

Dem Himmel nah, ist nah sie dem Getriebe—
Drum deutsche ich sie ein: die Wesensliebe.

Das Wesen liebt der Chassid, liebend hält
Er's fest in Gott, im Menschen, in der Welt.

Die Wesensliebe überall zu suchen
Ging ich einst aus, um sie getreu zu buchen.

In diesem Buch vereint ist, was ich fand,
Ein Traum, ein wahr Geschehn, ein Heimatsland.

HASIDUT

—Is *Hasidut* surely to be named piety?
—I have learned to know earthly traits in it.

—So is it to be called kindness and tender-heartedness?
—Then you bind it all too much into time.

Near to heaven, near to the bustle of earth—
Therefore I translate it: love of the creature.

The Hasid loves the creature, lovingly he holds it
Fast in God, in man, in the world.

To seek love of the creature everywhere
I once set out faithfully to put it in a book.

In this book is united what I found,
A dream, a true event, a homeland.

RELIGIOUS EDUCATION

IF FAITH signifies not a mere conviction or certainty that something is but a binding oneself to something, an involvement of one's own person, an immeasurably binding venture, then there is no education for faith. But there is an education to this insight as to what faith is and what it is not. One can lead no one to real faith, but one can show another the face of real faith, show it so clearly that he will not henceforth confuse faith with its artful ape, "religious" feeling. And one can teach him *with what* one believes when one really believes: with the lived moment and ever again with the lived moment. But if anywhere, this education begins in the realm of the deepest self-recollection: there where one questions himself, decides, and puts himself to the test.

ON THE SCIENCE OF RELIGION

A GREAT German scholar, the philologist Albrecht Dieterich, once stated that there exists "no science* of the divine, only the development of human thinking about the divine"; there exists "from a scholarly standpoint no divine revelation, only development of human thinking about divine revelation."† The subject of the science of religion, according to this view, is religion.

But religion is not human thought about the divine; it becomes that only where and in so far as it goes over into theology. (Theology is the thought of a religion, its thought about the divine; there exists no general theology, always only the thought of a religion—theistic, pantheistic, etc. "Theology" is in truth an "unfree" metaphysics.) Religion is rather the relationship of the human to the divine. This relationship, regarded in the reality of the religious life, is included in the reciprocity of the divine and the human. The science of religion detaches the relationship of the human to the divine as that alone which can be investigated by it, detaches this relationship from the reciprocity and observes it in itself. If this science knows what it does thereby, it acts legitimately, in the sense of the legitimacy of every striving for knowledge that does not overstep its normative limit but rather remains aware of this limit and allows its work to be codetermined by it. The limit which a legitimate science of religion has to re-

---

* The German word *"Wissenschaft"* applies to any branch of knowledge and not just to the natural sciences—M.F.

† *Verhandlungen des II. Internationalen Kongresses für Allgemeine Religionsgeschichte* (Basel, 1905), p. 76.

main aware of in a fashion codeterminate of its work is the line of break that arose when it detached the relationship of the human to the divine from the reciprocity of the divine and the human. What takes place on the other side of this line it cannot include in its research; but it must include in its research the fundamental and continual knowledge that the reality character of its subject is only to be comprehended from consideration of the limit as such, *i.e.,* only from paying attention to the fact of the total reciprocity. Without comprehension of the reality character of its subject, not merely the subject but also its work on it becomes fictitious: all work of such a "science of religion" by making a senseless game out of the meaning of our lives remains itself an unbinding game.

In place of the misleading assertion that scientifically there is no divine revelation, therefore, this truth must step forth: the divine revelation can certainly never be an object of scientific research, but it is its real limit, the reality as its limit, and thereby its mainstay, its strength-giving origin, and its direction-giving goal.

Therefore, the science of religion is so much the more genuinely grounded, the more directly it can join itself to a living knowledge about revelation. To this extent a science of religion which proceeds from the inner reality of a religion of revelation can provide a kind of knowledge that the general science of religion cannot provide. Yet the task of a Jewish, a Christian science of religion will be wholly misconstrued if it remains in the realm of Judaism, of Christianity, and compares all the phenomena of other religiousness with that of the one with which it is familiar, measures the value of the others by its own, identifies the particularity of its own religion with the essence of all religion and banishes all that is alien to it from the sphere of religious reality. Beyond this, often enough, the inner aspect of one's own religion is juxtaposed to the outer aspect of other religions. Rather precisely our proceeding from the inner reality of our own religion, in which our living knowledge of revelation is rooted, shall enable us to penetrate to the unique reality of the other religions and to do it justice—since we know this too, indeed, that the united revelation breaks into the multiplicity of the human.

He who compares the inner aspect of his own religion with the outer aspect of this same religion will be instructed by the knowledge of the distance between the two as to how much in the other religions, too, their inner reality may be removed from the outer aspect that first meets us and how great an exertion of penetration and making imaginatively present is needed in order to come so close to this inner reality that we can legitimately deal with it scientifically. Of course, a boundary is also set for us here: the innermost reality of a religion, its all-holiest and all-realest, is only accessible to the consecrated. This boundary is in the final truth identical with that limit of the sciences: its mystery, the mystery of the multiplicity of the religions, is ultimately identical with the mystery of the duality of religion and science. The solution of this mystery, the overcoming of that multiplicity and duality, means the messianic world.

PHILOSOPHICAL
AND RELIGIOUS WORLD VIEW

THE VERB "to know" is used in a twofold sense: 1. According to the customary manner of speaking "to know" means, in effect, "to regard a thing as an object." At the bottom of it lies the relation of subject and object. (Philosophical world view.) 2. The verb to know has another sense in the Biblical sentence: "Adam *knew* his wife Eve." Here the relationship of being to being is meant in which the real *knowing of I and Thou* takes place, but not of subject to object. This knowing lays the foundation for the religious world view.

The first kind of knowing, the philosophical, is, of course, an indispensable necessity and duty of human existence. It guarantees the continuity of thought through which man has acquired his special position in nature; it lays the foundation for the cohesion of the experience and of the thought of mankind. But it is purchased at the price of renouncing the lasting I-Thou relationship; in particular, it can found no community. Subject and object are necessary artifacts of the act of thought. The living to-each-other does not know this division. The man who knows in the subject-object relation, hence before all the philosophical man, begins therefore by looking away from his *concrete situation*. Philosophy is the application of this subject-object relation to the total connection of being. It is grounded in the belief in the all powerfulness of thinking; it totalizes the partial, thinking's function as a part. It was Kant's pathfinding discovery that in subject-object knowing, hence in philosophical-scientific knowing, we only know that which has been formed beforehand in our categories of thought. Phenomenology too regards the contents of thought in its determination as content of thought; it is the praxis to Kant's theory of knowledge.

But the great systems are not therefore fictitious: they are announcements of *real* thought relationships to existing being. But they can only become possible through the re-establishment of the object-subject relation, hence through entering into the mortal duty of knowledge. Being, in so far as it metes itself out to the human thought contents, is *also* in the thinking of man, and the knowing spirit is a spark of the *pneuma,* even though a detached spark—spirit in the attitude of self-contemplation. For for all our duty to this thinking it remains the case: in the act of looking away, *all* scientific and philosophical thinking tears asunder not merely the wholeness of the concrete person but also God and man from each other.

The science of history, for example, is driven by necessity as though there were no working of God. When the acknowledgment of God's working in history is taken seriously, the science of history is not possible, namely in the situation of taking seriously. There is a knowledge of faith about the working of God in history but not within philosophy and scholarship: no faith exists within the attitude of scholarship. The history of religion does not have to do with the working of God but with religion as a *human* expression of life, not with the divine side of history but with the material of religious experience. The legitimacy of scholarship is grounded on the fact that it includes nothing from beyond systematic knowledge in the scholarly observation. But the scholar is allowed and charged with the glimpse of the limit, the looking out to the concrete situation and to the concrete divine working. If science has this genuine glimpse as its limit, if it thus knows what it does and does not overstep its limit, then it does not, of course, lose the problematic of the subject-object relation. But it still remains installed within an integral part of the relationship of I and Thou and avoids the particular fall into sin of the thinker of our time: the false autonomy, the hardening before God.

Beyond this limit of philosophy and scholarship, there arises single and underivable the unique reality of the world *concretum* presented me by God: the continual creation in each moment. This religious situation which accosts me is not foreseeable and foreknowable, hence cannot be caught in any religious world continuity and in any religious world view. I must *enter* into the religious situation, must *hold my* ground in the face of the world *concretum* presented to me. If philosophy, even every philosophy of religion is directed to and reflects on the object-subject relationship as Being, then religion is not directed to the relationship but to the Thou; it *practices* the living relationship of I-Thou.

How then do scientific-philosophical statements differ from religious ones?

Every scientific-philosophical statement stands under the law of contradiction: A is not equal to not-A. The religious statement simply does not stand under the law of contradiction. When theologians believe that they can make statements about God under the law of contradiction, they are not acting from the standpoint of religion. This holds even for the negative theology of Karl Barth: it is not permissible to say God is the Wholly Other without God also at the same time being recognized as the Wholly Near, the intimate. The religious situation is simply the abode of the *lived complexio oppositorum*. In the religious situation it is not permissible to say, "God is transcendent and not immanent" or the reverse; he is both. Every religious statement is a risk that may be risked when it takes place in the living *complexio oppositorum,* as a pointing to the situation in which God only shows himself biographically. Even faith is not faith that something is, not knowledge with a content, but factual event, lived life in dialogue: being addressed by word and sign, answering by doing and not-doing, by holding one's ground and being responsible in the lived everyday. The religious statement is the witness of this dialogue.

If the philosophical-scientific man speaks of the unknown mystery, then he always does so only as of the mystery knowable "in itself." The religious man knows only the mystery to whose nature the inscrutability belongs and to which only standing firm and involvement open access.

This immediate relationship means for the person the becoming whole of the soul. For only with a whole soul can one enter into the concrete. What characterizes our present condition of stress are the various forces of the soul becoming autonomous. But this immediate relationship to the mystery also means the becoming whole of the spiritual life: the individual spiritual spheres which have become independent *unite* when a genuine religious communal life again exists. The separation of the spiritual spheres has led to the many modern idols. But the dreadfulness of our situation lies in the fact that religion is regarded as *one* aspect of the spiritual world. Any martyrdom is more conducive to religion than this freedom to operate as one of the spiritual spheres next to others. Much less still, of course, is religion a synthesis of the spiritual spheres.

Concretely seen, the contemporary so-called "world views" ["*Weltanschauungen*"] present themselves to us as systems of flight, as securities against the duty of really beholding the world. But genuine religious *comprehending* of the world includes: proceeding from the present concrete being and situation of the person; entering into the present world situation as the speech of God to me; beholding all that is presented to me and its origination, its being created together with me ("We see the things in God"); and the responsible answer of man, the loving hallowing of the things in the everyday. *To this real relation, however, one can be educated.*

From the Discussion

The religions speak to one another of a common *abstractum* (congress of religions); but I believe in the common *concretum,* the coming together, the kingdom of God. From the common *concretum* one can, one may, one must speak. And that is then the genuine speech. Its criterion is: it does not stream out of *one* independent province of the inner life but out of the totality: it does not *withold* itself. In other words, one can only speak on the foundation of *confessing,* not confessing religion, confessing *oneself*! Philosophical thinking is the self-contemplation of the human spirit. It assures the connection of thought of man, assures that men understand one another in conceptual speech. But in conceptual speech lies the tension of falling away from one another: we do not mean the same things by our concepts, and so basically we do not understand one another. Therefore philosophy too is incapable of forming community. But it is inexorably necessary as a phenomenon belonging to the way of redemption.

The "vision" is the first disengagement from the I-Thou relationship. The man in I-Thou "beholds" nothing else than what he sees with his senses: the world in God, not the face of God. But because he is taken into the duty of knowing, he passes through a condition in which the relationship of I-Thou is still illuminated but at the same time the detachment begins: no longer I-Thou knowing, *not yet* subject-object knowing.

The false autonomy is the absolute life of man in self-enjoyment, in concerning himself with himself. The consequence of this is the becoming independent of the spiritual spheres. It is then held, for example, that aesthetics has nothing to do with ethics, politics nothing to do with religion; the politician can be a pious man and yet engage in immoral politics, etc. But there also exists a genuine, God-willed autonomy: the life in all seriousness of man, from the human, to God: an act that works in the sense of obedience and proves itself obedient.

In revelation something happens to man from a side that is not man, not soul, not world. Revelation does not take place in man and is not to be explained through any psychologism. He who speaks of "the God in his breast" stands on the outermost rim of being: one cannot, one may not live from there. Revelation does not gush forth from the unconscious: it is mastery over the unconscious. Revelation comes as a might from without, but not in such a way that man is a vessel that is filled or a mere mouthpiece. Rather the revelation seizes the human elements that are at hand and recasts them: it is the *pure shape of the meeting.*

ON THE SITUATION
OF PHILOSOPHY

IT IS NOW the right time again to take philosophy with the highest seriousness.

The prevailing functionalizing of the concept of truth threatens to disintegrate the human spirit, which can no longer endure when it loses faith in the truth. This threatening ruin is only to be met by posing anew from the beginning the question concerning the truth. But this posing anew should not be undertaken in the way it has been in a significant attempt of our time, that of Martin Heidegger in his recent publications on the problem of truth. Heidegger rightly postulates that we must not proceed from the truth as an "agreement of the representation with the object," but from truth as an inherent property of Being, its "unconcealment." But the fruits of this insight slip from our hands if, as Heidegger does, we relate the unconcealment simply to man and his essence as though Being sent man forth in order to attain to adequate openness through him. It can neither be the mandate nor the privilege of this hour of the hardest test to cast off the burden of the conceptual conscience that the critical self-knowledge of man has laid on us, as though it were one ultimately not in agreement with us.

The way of post-Cartesian thought has led us in particular over three stations of ground-breaking critique, over each of which the prohibition against turning back stands unmistakably written: the discoveries of the way in which our knowledge is bound to the historical nature of our existence (Vico), to the forms of our perception (Kant), and to the sociologically and psychologically determined diversity of being of the

136

knowing individual (the modern social- and psychoanalysis). The manifold theoretical and practical pragmatism of our time has, of course, perverted the critical insights thus won into a—biologically or even crudely utilitarian-based—stripping of the concept of truth both of its value and its reality. But this successful misuse must not tempt us to treat the great way of critical discoveries as unauthoritative and to presume to begin anew with a precritical, ostensibly in itself unassailable, conception of truth. It is hopelessly illusory to wish to set in opposition to the dogmatically absolutized thesis of conditionedness an axiomatic teaching of the unconditioned. The light of the truth inherent in Being breaks up in the human spirit and becomes manifest to the world in such brokenness, and just in it, hence specifically inadequate.

Man denies this reality peculiar to him when he declares himself to be the "illumination" of Being. As his spirit allows nothing of the primal light to pass through unbroken, so what is broken here is nowhere to be brought together. But with this prismatically colored brightness another specific truth, at once possibility and task, has come into being, a human truth. In this hour of the fate of the spirit there can no longer be a question of voting for the adequacy and against the inadequacy of human thought, as little as the other way round, but rather of determining and arbitrating the relation of the two and the limitation of each by the other. The future competence of the philosophizing man depends upon his knowing the conditionality and the unconditionality of his thinking *in one* and in such encompassing to fulfill the personal devotion of the undivided knowing creature to the Being of existing being.

HEALING THROUGH MEETING

A MAN who follows an intellectual profession must pause time after time in the midst of his activity as he becomes aware of the paradox he is pursuing. Each of these professions stands, indeed, on paradoxical ground. When he pauses, something important has already happened. But this happening only becomes significant if he does not content himself with taking such fleeting upheavals of a well-ordered world into the register of the memory. Again and again, not too long after the completion of the thus interrupted activity, he must occupy himself, in strenuous yet dispassionate reflection, with the actual problematic to which he has been referred. With the involvement of his living and suffering person, he must push forward to greater and still greater clarity of that paradox. Thus a spiritual destiny, with its peculiar fruitfulness, comes into being and grows—hesitating, groping, while groping wrestling, slowly overcoming, in overcoming succumbing, in succumbing illuminating. Such was the destiny of Hans Trüb.

But the particular profession that is in question here is the most paradoxical of all; indeed, it juts forth out of the sphere of the intellectual professions not less than do these ordered intellectual activities, taken together out of the totality of the professions. Certainly the lawyer, the teacher, the priest, no less the doctor of the body, each comes also to feel, as far as conscience genuinely infuses his vocation, what it means to be concerned with the needs and anxieties of men, and not merely, like the pursuer of a non-intellectual profession, with the satisfaction of their wants. But this man here, the psychotherapist, whose task is to be the watcher and healer of sick souls, again and again confronts the naked abyss of man, man's abysmal lability. This troublesome appendage had been thrown into the bargain when that process unknown to nature was acquired, which may be characterized in the specific sense as the psychic.* The psychotherapist meets the situation, moreover, not like the priest, who is armed with sacred possessions of divine grace and holy word, but as a mere person equipped only with the tradition of his science and the theory of his school. It is understandable enough that he strives to objectivize the abyss that approaches him and to convert the raging "nothing-else-than-process" into a thing that can, in some degree, be handled. Here the concept of the unconscious, manifoldly elaborated by the schools, affords him invaluable help. The sphere in which this renowned concept possesses reality is located, according to my understanding, beneath the level where human existence is split into physical and psychical phenomena. But any of the contents of this sphere can in any moment enter into the dimension of the introspective, and thereby be explained and dealt with as belonging to the psychic province.

On this paradoxical foundation, laid with great wisdom and art, the psychotherapist now practices with skill and also with success, generally, too, with the assistance of the patient, whom the tranquilizing, orienting, and to some extent integrating procedure for the most part pleases. Until, in certain cases, a therapist is terrified by what he is doing because he begins to suspect that, at least in such cases, but finally, perhaps, in all, something entirely other is demanded of him. Something incompatible with the economics of his profession, dangerously threatening, indeed, to his regulated practice of it. What is demanded of him is that he draw the particular case out of the correct methodological objectification and

---

* By this nothing else is meant than the series of phenomena that opens itself to the introspective activity.

himself step forth out of the role of professional superiority, achieved and guaranteed by long training and practice, into the elementary situation between one who calls and one who is called. The abyss does not call to his confidently functioning security of action, but to the abyss, that is to the self of the doctor, that selfhood that is hidden under the structures erected through training and practice, that is itself encompassed by chaos, itself familiar with demons, but is graced with the humble power of wrestling and overcoming, and is thus ready to wrestle and overcome ever anew. Through his hearing of this call there erupts in the most exposed of the intellectual professions the crisis of its paradox. The psychotherapist, just when and because he is a doctor, will return from the crisis to his habitual method, but as a changed person in a changed situation. He returns to it as one to whom the necessity of genuine personal meetings in the abyss of human existence between the one in need of help and the helper has been revealed. He returns to a modified method in which, on the basis of the experiences gained in such meetings, the unexpected, which contradicts the prevailing theories and demands his ever-renewed personal involvement, also finds its place.

An example, sketched only in general outline, may serve here for clarification of what has been set forth and show something further concerning it.

A man saddles himself with guilt toward another and represses his knowledge of it. Guilt, this fundamental life occurrence, is only rarely discussed in the psychoanalytic literature, and then generally only in terms of its subjective side, and not within the circumference of the ontic reality between man and man; that is, only its psychological projection and its elimination through the act of repression appear to be relevant here. But if one recognizes the ontic, in fact, suprapersonal ontic character of guilt, if one recognizes, therefore, that guilt is not hidden away inside the human person, but that the human person stands, in the most real way, in the guilt that envelops him, then it also becomes clear that to understand the suppression of the knowledge of guilt as a merely psychological phenomenon will not suffice. It hinders the guilty man, in fact, from accomplishing the reconciliation whose ontic nature has, to be sure, been rather obscured by some discussions of moral philosophy and moral theology. It hinders him from thereby influencing the suprapersonal facts of the case through setting right the disturbance engendered in the human constellations—a setting right of which the "purification" of the soul is only the accompanying manifestation within the person. Reconciliation cannot take place merely in relation to the man toward whom one has become guilty (and who is perhaps dead), but in relation to all and each, according to the path of his individual life, according to his surroundings and his circumstances. What matters is only that, starting with the fact of guilt, life be lived as a reconciling, a making good.

Let us assume that the man who has repressed his knowledge of guilt falls into a neurosis. He now comes to the psychotherapist for healing. The therapist draws what is especially favored by him within the all-containing microcosmos of the patient—Oedipus complex or inferiority feeling or collective archetype—from the unconscious into the conscious, and then treats it according to the rules of his wisdom and art; guilt remains foreign to him or uninteresting. In one case of which I am thinking in particular, a woman took another woman's husband, later suffered the same loss herself, then "crept away into her soul," only to be visited and unsettled by vagrant pains. The analyst (a well-known disciple of Freud) succeeded so thoroughly in "healing" that the pain fully ceased, the patient "came forth out of the soul" and lived her life to the end amid an abundance of agreeable and, to her mind, friendly social relationships: that incessant and highly painful reminder of the unreconciled, the disturbed relation-to-being that must be set right, was eradicated. I call this successful cure the exchange of hearts. The artificial heart, functioning entirely satisfactorily, no longer feels pain; only one of flesh and blood can do that.*

To the psychotherapist who has passed through this crisis of the paradox of his vocation, such "healing" is barred. In a decisive hour, together with the patient entrusted to and trusting in him, he has left the closed room of psychological treatment in which the analyst rules by means of his systematic and methodological superiority and has stepped forth with him into the air of the world where self is exposed to self. There, in the closed room where one probed and treated the isolated psyche according to the inclination of the self-encapsulated patient, the patient was referred to ever-deeper levels of his inwardness as to his proper world; here outside, in the immediacy of one human confronting another, the encapsulation must and can be broken through, and a transformed, healed relationship must and can be opened to the person who is sick in his relations to otherness—to the world of the other which he cannot remove into his soul. A soul is never sick alone, but there is always a between-ness also, a situation between it and another existing being. The psychotherapist who has passed through the crisis may now dare to touch on this.

This way of frightened pause, of unfrightened reflection, of personal involvement, of rejection of security, of unreserved stepping into relationship, of the bursting of psychologism, this way of vision and of risk is that which Hans Trüb trod. After repeated wrestlings with the word for the unfamiliar, he has set forth his findings ever more maturely, ever more adequately, until its maturest and most adequate expression in this work, which he was not able to finish. His foot can no

---

* For a more detailed discussion of this particular example (the case of "Melanie") and an extensive discussion of ontic, or "existential," guilt, see Martin Buber, *The Knowledge of Man,* ed. with Introductory Essay by Maurice Friedman (New York: Harper Torchbooks, 1966), "Guilt and Guilt Feelings" trans. by Maurice Friedman, pp. 128 ff.—M.F.).

longer push on, but the path is broken. Surely there will not be wanting men like him—awake and daring, hazarding the economics of the vocation, not sparing and not withholding themselves, risking themselves—men who will find his path and extend it further.

ON THE PSYCHOLOGIZING
OF THE WORLD

WHAT WE are speaking of is something that does not exist outside of us but within our lives. From out of our lives it must ever again be set right, from out of our lives testimony to it must ever again be given if we wish to penetrate into the depths of the subject.

"Psychologizing of the world" is the inclusion of the world in the soul, the transference of the world into the soul, but not just any such transference but only that which goes so far that the essential is thereby disturbed. This essential is the facing of I and world. That the world faces me and that between us the real happens, this essential basic relation from which our life receives its meaning is injured if the world is so far removed within the soul that its non-psychic reality is obliterated, that this fundamental relation of I to world ceases to be able to be a relation of I to Thou. (In place of world we can also say here Being.) After this essential disturbance the world is perhaps only something in me with which I can certainly concern myself, as with other things in me to which, however, I cannot legitimately, cannot in full truth say *Thou*.

This fact of psychologizing can also be called by a philosophical expression, psychologism. What is in question here, however, is not a world view, as psychologism is otherwise, but a fact that exists in almost every man of today.

The reality in which the non-perverted man finds himself is the reality of an immediate connection of I and world, a connection, however, which signifies no fusion, but a connection of relation. It is founded upon the I and the world as entities clearly separate from each other. The arch of rela-

144

tionship rises, as it were, on these two clearly individual pillars. This natural relation is easily obscured in the course of development, on the one side in that human thought removes the world into the soul (cosmic phenomena are grasped as psychic, they are a function, dependent upon the soul of man), on the other side in that the soul is removed into the world and appears as its product, as something that has grown out of it, as understandable on the basis of its evolution.

This double game of human thought is furthered by one fact: namely that however separately the two pillars stand opposite each other, there still exists a mutual inclusion of I and world. *Psychologism* in its easiest form regards the world as an idea. *Cosmologism* regards the soul as an element, a product of the world. In the face of this fact, we must still say: The world is, of course, also my *idea, i.e.,* I *also* possess it as idea; only what is essential in it does not enter into my idea—the world's character of being does not enter into it. And conversely, if the soul is conceived from the standpoint of the world, what is essential in the soul (the I) remains outside, is not included in the world. (Instead of speaking substantively of the I, we can also say the I's character as self.) It is so that this mutual inclusion, soul–world and world–soul, exists; but the essence of the one and of the other remain thereby untouched.

Now the question arises: are these two aspects which at a certain level of development of man appear on the scene and belong to each other, are they things between which we must choose, are they opposites for which no third thing exists that overarches this opposition, overcomes it? Must this rendering being fictitious exist, although a relation of the world to the soul is thereby made impossible? I do not believe so. Today, to be sure, we can only hint at this third that can liberate us from the two; it is not yet graspable even in the form of a provisional image.

The perspective that sees the inclusion of I and world as a whole and embeds this whole in the real being (the perspective that sees the reality so truly that this inclusion has its place in it), is a greater apprehension of reality than that to which we are accustomed. The reality into which the concepts of the psychic and the cosmic can enter is the *pneumatic reality* (according to a religious valuation). This reality understood as existing being, as existing being into which all that is psychic and all that is cosmic and all that is opposite and all that is inclusive of the two is embedded, this *ontologism* we can, with all foresight and self-limitation, set up for a moment as a third to the two—psychologism and cosmologism—a third which unites them. But careful! Exact knowledge of the limitation of what one says! What we are discussing is a problem, not an answer. Perhaps there are, for all that, hints of an answer or presentiments in it.

The Concept of the Soul: Is man really composed of soul and body? Does man really feel himself consisting of two kinds of things. Not *I!* Naturally two aspects exist, I perceive myself by my senses as well as from within me without my senses. But these are only two ways of seeing oneself. Are they really two kinds of things? From where does this division arise? From the fact of death and our relation to it. We are inclined to take the edge off death. We are inclined to say that this duality just simply comes apart. But we *know* of death only that it is the end of our conceivable being. We probably must also know, however, that we cannot die; yet we may not make the not-being-able-to-die conceptual otherwise than that it is the mystery itself, that it takes place in the mystery. But nowhere here do we find a legitimization of the division.

Nonetheless we know of psychic phenomena—thinking, feeling, willing, etc.—what are they? Are they like the body? Are the physical and the psychic alike in that the latter, *like* the body, belongs to the I as long as life is preserved? And, really, *there* is a going apart.

If we grasp the body I-wise and the soul I-wise, then they are only two aspects. But is not one of these interior aspects beyond the I?—Yes, indeed. If we regard more deeply what we call the psychic phenomena in their essence, then we find that all of them and their connection point to something that cannot be understood from the standpoint of the I, that transcending even the phenomena of solitude, of apparent individuality, in reality point to something beyond the individual. Even though a great number of phenomena appear thus, as though they stood outside of the relationship between the I and the other, these phenomena also have only arisen dynamically from out of the fact of relationship and are only comprehensible through this fact.

Concept of the Spirit: Spirit and soul are both, as it were, planes of relationship. Neither is to be understood as the I; they are to be regarded as various forms of relationship in its being removed to the I. Soul is to be understood from the relationship between man and world, spirit from the relationship between man and that which is not world, between man and the Being that does not manifest itself in the world, that does not enter into the worldly manifestation. But both, soul and spirit, are not to be understood from the isolated individual, not to be understood as the *I,* but only from the relationship between I and worldly or nonworldly being. Characteristic of both is the dynamic, *i.e.,* that they stand in a continually developing double movement, in the unfolding or realization of the relationship and in the I's withdrawing-into-itself or being-withdrawn from the relationship (The spirit is different in this from the soul; the spirit points to something from which it stems, points to something new which arises ever again, what exists from of old in a nonindividuated, unconditioned manner. That is too delicate to be able to say more about it.) The character of the soul as I is thereby broken: in so far as the soul is comprehended as I, it is comprehended in amputation, in abstraction, not in the whole existence.

"Psychologizing of the world" thus means abstraction, attempt at a complete detachment of the soul from its basic character of relationship. This derives from the fact that the spirit in its condition of highest differentiation is inclined to bend back on itself, i.e., that the spirit to the extent of its individuation is inclined to forget, to deny that it does not exist *in* man (in I), but between man and what is not man (what is not world). Then Being is psychologized, installed within the soul of man. The world no longer confronts the soul. That is the soul-madness of the spirit. In place of the soul, which is a plane of relationship between man and world, an all-penetrating substance is created: all is transformed into soul. This fact is the true fall. Here first the fall takes place.

How does psychologism arise? We distinguish between philosophical and naïve psychologism.

Philosophical Psychologism: It is the foundation of the philosophical disciplines (that which determines the methods, lays the ground for the criteria). It is fundamental today even in cases where apparently another starting point can be or is chosen. Basically one ever again tries to go back to what he regards as the real, the undeniable, to the psychological. ("I do not mean something that exists outside the soul.") Even metaphysical views are psychologically legitimized. We are told to what psychic functions they correspond. It is also thus in the ethical, in the aesthetic realm. For example, in the aesthetic it is forgotten that we enter *into* a world when we go to the work of art, that we really come into something new; this *work,* this being is absorbed and it is asserted that it exists in us. One does not recognize that it *is* and that beforehand it just was not possessed by us. To transpose the relation into the receiving subject means to destroy the being.

Naïve Psychologism: There is remarkably little awareness of this. Man always imagines everything as happening through and in him. "The landscape is a state of the soul," says Amiel. That is a malformation of the genuine nature feeling. Something *other* is, but one forgets the duality and experiences the relationship so strongly that this is felt more strongly than the existence of the two individuals. Thus also God is played with

(Rilke). In the Youth Movement the relation between man and reality is spoken of, but in so doing men are all inclined to regard this as something tied up with their person; all the conceptions in the youth movement take on a certain "my" character. (For example: discussion of a tragic occurrence between men is ever again interlaced with statements which begin, "*My* kind . . . *My* blood . . . *My* destiny, etc.") Somewhat similar is the fact that many men are determined in their inner focus by how they appear to other men, that they all refer back to the image that they produce in others. They do not live from the core out, not to the other from their own center, but from the image that they produce in others.*

And the erotic: almost throughout only differentiated self-enjoyment. The other man is not made present in his life, not accepted as the other life with its right. What is elementally perceived is what takes place in one's own soul. Even the attempts at the spiritual life, the religious life are soaked through with the same poison. The term expressionism is indicative: the important is seen not in the communication between me and the form to which I strive but in the expression of what takes places *in me*. Thereby the real connexion is destroyed. Only out of the belief in the not-I can I enter into a connexion; I must walk toward the other, beholding, hearkening, fulfilling him.

Active Form of Psychologism: Relation of present-day man to himself: How does man perceive himself? First of all through *self-experience:* this is met with in the natural growth of consciousness. What ascends between me and myself and becomes conscious in this level of relationship of the soul (between me and the world) in its dynamic (coming to each other, stripping apart, becoming alone) is self-experience gained through a natural growth of consciousness. Here no

---

* This is the origin of the typology of "being and seeming" which Buber later develops in *The Knowledge of Man,* "Elements of the Interhuman"—M.F.

willfulness interferes. Secondly, *self-observation:* that is an interference; it wills to further the growth and thwarts it. It does not lead to deeper self-experience but disintegrates it. What one seemingly experiences thus is not the reality but something distorted. It is not experience but belaboring. One can only experience without willfulness. It is similar with *experience of the soul* (a happiness, a present, it gives an artist greatness) *and observation by the soul* (can be industriously exercized, yet yields only talent).

Scientific Form of Psychologism: It expresses itself in the analytical method, more exactly "analyticism," which applies this method as universally valid, which no longer knows, therefore, that it is a method and only *provisionally* usable and must always be ready to be given up. When the analysis longs for synthesis, it is not thus. When the man knows, now I must do this, I must, for example, seek a motive although I know that no motive exists, I must, for example, dissect the life of the soul although it is a unity, that is not analyticism. In this wise restriction, I would gladly emphasize this, I have often encountered the analytical method precisely in the representatives of the direction prevailing here* as true scientific method.

Here another word about the problematic of the province of psychotherapy. The sicknesses of the soul are sicknesses of relationship. They can only be treated completely if I transcend the realm of the patient and add to it the world as well. If the doctor possessed superhuman power, he would have to try to heal the relationship itself, to heal in the "between." The doctor must know that really he ought to do that and that only his boundedness limits him to the one side.

Psychology is the investigation of the soul in a set abstraction from the world (similar to the way that plane geometry deals with planes, although only solid objects exist). The limit of psychology is there where this set (assumed) abstrac-

---

* See Explanatory Comments, 1., p. 240.

tion abolishes itself on reality, where it touches on reality, on the relationship. What *share* can psychology have *in the overcoming of psychologism?* We can only grasp this overcoming if we understand that psychologism is a marginal phenomenon. This marginal phenomenon clearly develops into self-contradiction. If psychologism becomes so intensified that the man can simply no longer bring his capacity for external relationship (the inborn Thou*) to others, to the world, if his strength of relationship recoils backward into the I, if he has to encounter himself, if the double ever again appears to him, then that state exists that I call self-contradiction.† Attempt at flight is pseudo-religiousness (the double possesses a religious meaning). This phenomenon is the place of the turning.‡

Community in a time like ours can only happen out of breakthrough, out of turning. Only the need aroused by the uttermost sundering, the marginal phenomenon, provides the motive force for this. Does psychology, the true, the genuine psychology, have a function in this? Only from the standpoint of psychology is the problematic of individuation manifest. Only when it comes to its borders, does it come on the unpsychological. Through the self-suspension of the shut-off levels of individuation, psychology can lead to a genuine apprehension of community and—deed. Genuine community begins in a time like this with the discovery of the metapsychic character of reality and rests upon the belief in this reality.

The *empirical community* is a dynamic fact. It does not take away from man his solitude but fills it, makes it positive. It thereby deepens the consciousness of responsibility of

---

* See Explanatory Comments, 2., pp. 240 f.

† See Explanatory Comments, 3., p. 241.

‡ "The turning" is a basic term not only in *I and Thou* but throughout Buber's thought from his earliest to his latest writings. It goes back to the *teshuvah* of the Hebrew Bible—the call of the prophets to turn back to God with one's whole existence, including one's relations to one's fellowmen, one's community, other peoples, and the world of nature—M.F.

the individual—the place of responsibility is man's becoming solitary. The community does not have its meaning in itself. It is the abode where the divine has not yet consumed itself, the abode of the coming theophany. If one knows this, then one also knows that community in our time must ever again miscarry. The monstrous, the dreadful phenomenon of psychologism so prevails that one cannot simply bring about healing, rescue with a single blow. But the disappointments belong to the way. There is no other way than that of this miscarrying. That is the way of faithful faith.

THE UNCONSCIOUS

1

THERE IS a story in Confucius' Analects about a disciple who spent some time at the court of one of the kings "clearing up concepts." As long as they are unclear, everything in the kingdom is doubtful. Concepts become problematic because they do not show a concrete context that can be controlled. Every abstraction must stand the test of being related to a concrete reality without which it has no meaning. This revision of concepts entails a necessary destruction if the new generation is not to be the lifelong slave of tradition.

The History of the Unconscious: What *Leibnitz* says about "small imperceptible perceptions" is near the unconscious, but it is not the same thing. He is talking about elements of the soul-process. *Plotinus* had a clear doctrine of the unconscious: "We do not know all that occurs in any part of the soul just by the fact of its occurring. We know it only when it has penetrated the whole soul." (Fourth Ennead, 8,8) "For it is very possible that even without being conscious of having something one has it in himself and even in a form more effective than if he knew it." (Fourth Ennead, 4,4) "The consciousness seems to obscure the actions that it perceives and only when they occur without it, are they purer, more effective, and more vital." (First Ennead, 4,10) The unconscious is a vital force in me, and if I try to make it conscious, I may spoil it. I cannot in utter seriousness accept the term soul.

Consciousness has degrees. The penetration of the whole soul is not necessary for consciousness.

Nicholas Cusanus does not use the term, but he speaks about different modes of divine participation in our existence and this corresponds to different degrees of self-knowledge.

Leibnitz's views find their best exposition in his preface to *Nouveaux Essais:* "In every moment in our inner being there is an infinite multitude of perceptions that are not accompanied by apperception and reflection but represent only changes in the soul itself—changes of which we are not conscious because these impressions are either too feeble or too many or too uniform so that they do not show sufficient marks of distinctions. Nevertheless, they can have their effect in unison with other perceptions, and they can be valid in the totality of impressions if only in a somewhat vague and indistinct mode." This is near to the modern psychological concept of the unconscious, but unlike Plotinus it is a description rather than a theory. Nevertheless, the influence of the idea of Leibnitz was very strong. *Novalis'* remarks on the unconscious depend on Leibnitz and so do those of other German romantics.

In German philosophy *Hamann,* the antagonist of Kant, has much to say on this subject. In the eighteen forties *C. G. Carus,* the father of modern psychology, builds his psychology on just this: "The key to the knowledge of the nature of the life of the conscious soul lies in the region of unconsciousness." He means we cannot understand any conscious phenomenon without understanding its unconscious basis. *Eduard von Hartmann* made of the unconscious the solution to the riddle of the world. Instead of the will of his master Schopenhauer he made the unconscious the movement of creation. He trivialized Schopenhauer.

Freud knew Carus and Von Hartmann. He gave a clear definition—physiological but not biological. Freud was an enraged antivitalist, a real mechanist. One does not find the vitalist current of Bergson in Freud.

The main argument Freud repeatedly mentions as opposed to his doctrine of the unconscious is that the unconscious cannot be psychical because the psychic is conscious. In opposition to this Freud stated that there are occurrences in human beings beyond conscious knowledge but dynamically effective. This is a curious, false alternative—between the unconscious as *only* physiological or *only* psychic. Certain unconscious processes functioned in such a way that they had the property of mind.

REED: It was a tautologous consequence of the popular definition of mind.

DR. EDITH WEIGERT: Freud believed in the division of mind.

BUBER: Just so. Is is one or the other? The unconscious to Freud is not a phenomenon, but it has effects on phenomena. This is not a substantive dualism but a functional one. Despite the revolution in the teachings of Jung, in all his writings too, he puts the unconscious into the *psychic* category and so in all modern psychology. What is the radical difference between physical and psychical phenomena and what is the criterion for subsuming any phenomenon here or here? And why cannot the subconscious be subsumed in one place or the other? Not only the distinguishing of two substances, as in all philosophy, but even the distinguishing of two functional realms is not sufficient.

The *physical* and the *psychical* represent two radically different modes of knowing: either the senses or "inner sense." What is the radical difference between phenomena given by the outer senses and those given by the inner sense? Feeling —pure psychic process in time—cannot be found as physical. My memory retains the process but by a new process in time. Physiology deals with things that are to be found, psychology with things that are not to be found. The assumption that the unconscious is either body or soul is unfounded. The unconscious is a state out of which these two phenomena have not yet evolved and in which the two cannot be at all distinguished from each other. The unconscious is our being itself and these two are evolving out of it again and again in every moment. In order to become phenomena, the unconscious must dissociate itself—one of the methods of this dissociation is analytical psychology.

Not everything that is, is a phenomenon. The region of a phenomenon is limited. The psychic is pure process in time. There are meeting points between the physical and the psychic—conscious ones—but we must distinguish between the two realms. Psychic process *cannot* go on in the brain whatever the relation between the two may be. *"Die Seele ist nicht befindlich."* In order to grasp the physical as a whole I need the category of space as well as time. But for the psychic I need time alone.

I mean what modern psychology means by the unconscious—this dynamic fact making itself felt by its effects, effects which the psychologist can explore. For example, if there *are* archetypes we learn something of them by their effects. The archetypes themselves, says Jung, can never be sensed, but they influence life in such and such a way that can only come out of this "anima." I don't contest at all that psychology is right in saying there are things that influence our life and that come out in certain conscious states. We cannot say anything about the unconscious in itself. It is never given to us. But we can deduce from certain conscious states that there must be certain things. The radical mistake of Freud was to think that he could have it and not have it. The psychoanalyst cannot understand the unconscious of the other, but he can understand the conscious of the other as a primary thing—there is immediate understanding between man and man. *Wilhelm Dilthey* tried to analyze *das Verstehen*—the understanding of one another.

2

MAURICE FRIEDMAN—summary and speculation: The basic distinction between the physical and the psychic, though not clear cut, does not follow into the unconscious, which is non-phenomenological and prior to the split between psychic and physical. Freud's logical error, followed by all schools of psychoanalysis, places the unconscious within the person alone. Hence reality is seen as psychic rather than interhuman.

BUBER: Most psychological schools, especially that of Jung, assume that there is a nonphenomenological yet psychical reality. This means the assumption of a rather mystical basis of reality. We know from continuous life experience only about being, comprehending the two directions and two kinds of phenomena. The assumption of a psyche that exists as something exists in space should be either a metaphor or an entirely metaphysical thesis about the nature of being for which we have no basis at all in experience. Freud remained in the last instance a radical physiologist. Jung dealt wrongly with the problem, and Freud did not deal with it at all. Freud takes these questions lightly till the end. Freud does not speak explicitly of the psyche but of what is "psychoate." He never defines it. Freud was a simplificator, just as in the social field Marx was before him, *i.e.,* one who places a general concept in place of the ever-renewed investigation of reality. A new aspect of reality is treated by the simplificator as the solution of one of the riddles of being. Fifty years of psychotherapeutic thought have been based on this dangerous manner of thinking. Now this period is at an end.

REED: Freud, like the positivists, was not concerned about such questions, but Freud has some explicit metapsychological theorizing.

BUBER: Yes, at the end, but he would not give up what went before and therefore could not accomplish anything thereby. Besides his school clung to his former theories. They had built a whole doctrine and practice on it. But it was a great attempt to grasp the problems in a philosophical manner—a tragic attempt. A thinker who begins anew without daring to begin anew in all earnest must fail. Some thinkers could only avoid it by leaving everything in the state of problems ever renewing themselves. This is the specific responsibility of the thinking man in the face of reality.

DR. TUCKER: Would you equate the psychic with consciousness?

BUBER: There are many degrees of consciousness. Therefore, if in a certain sphere there are so many spheres, I would rather not make it basic. But I cannot define what the psychic is. The main way of thought is again and again to criticize concepts and definitions and face them with a reality that those thinkers did not know about. I decline to define not only because I do not know, but also in the interests of this dynamic of thinking. But the psychic that is going on in this moment cannot be itself sufficiently an object to make a definition possible.

TUCKER: Would you equate the psychic with mind?

BUBER: The psychic we know directly without problem, but "mind" is an indispensable objectification.

DR. LESLIE FARBER:* One of the arguments Freud gives for the unconscious is post-hypnotic phenomena. The subject of the unconscious is usually one of suggestion, *i.e.,* the person will fall asleep and do so and so. And as we know well by now there is no identity between sleep and hypnosis.

BUBER: What in this hypnotized person is being influenced? Carus would say the psyche. This is just the doubtful point. I would say not the psyche but that nonphenomenal unconscious that dissociates itself into the physiological and psychological. Upon his waking out of hypnosis the first thing that happens is this dissociation. The first thing that happens, therefore, is the contact between the two states rather than the common sphere.

FARBER: I find something here that makes the forgetting of

---

* Dr. Leslie H. Farber was at that time Chairman of the Faculty of the Washington (D.C.) School of Psychiatry and was responsible for bringing Martin Buber to America to give the Fourth William Alanson White Memorial Lectures (now included in *The Knowledge of Man*) during the course of which these seminars took place—M.F.

dreams more understandable. One reason they leave so quickly unless they are objectivized in such fashion in psychic awareness is that they do not exist as such.

BUBER: Do we know dreams at all? *Have* we a dream as I have this glass? We have the work of shaping memory. But how can I accept this as the reality he dreamed rather than his attitude in relation to the "dream" that I can never know in itself. This is the first question. The second is that of the "content" of dreams and with it Freud's whole theory of repression. What is the main difference between the state of waking and the state of dreaming. We are inclined to think the rhythmical recurrence of dreams is analogous to the conscious state of the soul. Yet we cannot compare a dream to any other phenomenon. In the dream itself it seems we have a certain feeling of consciousness. Its relation to consciousness in psychic life is a real problem. What is the general connection between parts of conscious life? Something very different. Freud has not even tried to deal with these things. Sometimes when I am waking I make a violent effort to detach myself from the world of dreams and enter the common world of man (Heraclitus).*

Another question: Some contents that we have in conscious life appear again in dreams. What is the identity and nonidentity of the dream-object with that in waking life? A fourth question: As we all know, there is in conscious life an ordering force. Any morning anew when we awake a power begins to make us act and to live in a common cosmos. There is a hegemony. Nothing of this kind is going on in dreams. They have a certain continuity and connection of their own. What is the nature of this difference? A psychological theory of the dream is made terribly difficult by the fact that the dream is not given us as an experience or an object of investigation or something that can be compared with

---

* See Buber, *The Knowledge of Man*, "What Is Common to All," trans. by Maurice Friedman—M.F.

the conscious. In my old age I have not arrived at a state of equanimity about the dreams I have every night. Freud dealt with it as self-understood. The Taoists never ceased to think about the problem of dreams. The dream is a problem really neighboring that of death. Shakespeare's comparison is not metaphorical, for both are unknown by their very nature. We think we know the dream of our shaping memory, but there is a substrate that eludes us.

MOLLEGEN: Does the shaping memory exist in the dream too?

BUBER: That's a very different kind of shaping memory. In conscious life we can see a legend born in utter innocence. This may go on in dreams, but we cannot know it. There is no objective preservation of a dream whereas other memories have the check of other witnesses.

EDITH WEIGERT: The dream has much similarity with some productions of psychotics; both are disorganized.

BUBER: The human being in the condition of the ordered world does not tolerate something disordered.

WEIGERT: It is very important that we penetrate into his private world in order to break through the disorganization.

BUBER: Here is just the difference. You cannot try to come in touch with the dreamer. As soon as you succeed, there is no more dreaming. It is a dynamic difference.

WEIGERT: You can try to get in touch with the psychotic later when he is less anxious and better organized and this is what we do with the dreamer.

BUBER: No, I can try to come in touch with the schizophrenic. I cannot get in touch with a dreamer. The schizophrenic remains a schizophrenic and something in him becomes common. There is nothing common with the dreamer.

DR. WEININGER: Sometimes he comes out of sleep with something changed in his consciousness.

BUBER: He lies awake in a state of unusual lucidity, but this is passing from sleep into a state of lucidity. I remember and others have confirmed that there are nights of extraordinary lucidity without sleep. The solving of problems in sleep also occurs there. It is an extraordinary awakeness—much more than in the common world. This is not dream or sleep.

MRS. MARJORIE FARBER: Is a dream not like a work of art minus a conscious "creator"?

BUBER: Imagination is not bound to a certain connection of images. It is not responsible in relation to facts. It has its own laws, but it is not bound to a certain material. But the man remembering dreams would not change anything consciously, willingly. There is a tension of will not to change anything in the dream. In imagination I have a sense of dynamic process of which I am the subject. This distinguishes it from a flight of images. This latter is similar to the dream, but in the dream the single appearances are always connected with one another. The dream is epical—a series of events connected with one another—but these flights of images (faces) are entirely dissociated from one another. It has something in common with psychotic *Ideenflucht* (Binswanger).

MARGARET RIOCH: Are you equating the world of sleep and dreams with the unconscious?

BUBER: No, dreams are one of the forms of the unconscious. The so-called soul and the so-called body are not separated from one another, but there is a detached world. I don't differ at all from the analytical schools in this. I accept everything that they call unconscious as such. Some psychotic processes are this—as far as I cannot distinguish a psychic process.

FARBER: The dream is similar to some of the things that go on in psychosis.

KVARNES: In both you can observe it and not be part of it.

BUBER: You can have some dialogue with the schizophrenic.

KVARNES: The patient can drift in and out of psychosis in the course of one interview. In so far as he is psychotic you cannot reach him.

DR. CAMERON: In cases where therapy has progressed suc-cessfully there are cases where distance is lost between thera-pist and patient—dialogue. I have a bearded German patient, very ill, a schizophrenic with whom I had a false relation. Then he was struck by another patient and withdrew entirely into his own world. When I became aware that this kind of sharing was an essential factor in the relationship, then dis-tance reappeared. He told me his dream and he got better.

BUBER: There was a schizophrenic among my friends whose illness I followed for years. He had a wife with astonishing will power who wanted to see him recover once for all. I doubt if such is possible. If this man lives long enough, some of the same or similar events recur. In order to heal him, she visited him in the catatonic moments when he assumed atti-tudes, positions, and movements some of which are not pos-sible to a normal man. This woman tried and succeeded in imitating him and made the same movements as he. A curious thing then occurred. He let her into his particular world—took her in. Some schizophrenics want to introduce another person from the base common world of man into the particu-lar one—the only one of real value. The influence was posi-tive. Perhaps in the same measure as he let her in, he came out—he appreciated more a world common to the two of them. (Edith Weigert: *folie à deux*) About twenty-five years afterward, after this man for a series of years had been nor-mal—a professor in the university respected by all—I saw him and he told me of his wife that she does not venture to go out of her house or even leave her bed by day. The man was seemingly normal. We talked for some hours. But when I left, he told my wife that he had been very useful to the British through his connection with the stars.

Our common world is to the schizophrenic a world of illu-sions, conventions. Their particular world is the real one. They even have a double stream of memory.

DR. CAMERON: The absence of distance is characteristic of schizophrenia.

BUBER: In the dreams that we remember there is some-times an interposition of spaces, meaning that here things are going on and here other things, not intermingling. Here there are, so to speak, two planes, two space dimensions going on, one in the face of the other. Even more curious are appear-ances in time. I once had a dream in which at one moment I walked forward and a wind was blowing into my face, and I said to myself in the dream, "Ah, this is the other time." I felt not only the one line of time going on from birth to death, but also as if there were another line of time coming toward me, striking me. In reflection I thought, "Oh, this is the same thing with space as with time." In dreams there is a connec-tion of things entirely different from waking, but it exists. There was a time in my life when I knew very much of dreams and then less and less, so now it is only remembering. What Rank wrote on dreams is rather interesting.

WEIGERT: The decrease in interest in dreams is because the interpretation of dreams is an art.

BUBER: In its very reality the dream is inaccessible. The hypnotic dream is very different from the usual one. A cer-tain dream went on until in a moment I felt in the dream, "It is not as it should be—what now?" As if I were writing a story and thought of changing it. From this moment on the same scene occurred again and again with some variants. Finally, I succeeded in changing the last scene and it went on. This recurred many times. When awake I thought there is a certain moment of will in the dream though not felt as such in the dream.

DR. SMITH: What do you consider the implications you see in the unconscious and shaping memory of a dream?

BUBER: Dreams are not the best example because of the difficulty of making dreams a material of research.

SMITH: Dreams in practice are dealt with along lines you suggest more than the theories of dreams do.

BUBER: First I should advise to observe what the waking man does with the dream. In the last ten years or so I have the impression of a certain change in psychotherapeutic practice in which more and more therapists are not so confident that this or that theory is right and have a more "musical," floating relationship to their patient. The deciding reality is the therapist, not the methods. Without methods one is a dilettante. I am for methods, but just in order to use them not to believe in them. Although no doctor can do without a typology, he knows that at a certain moment the incomparable person of the patient stands before the incomparable person of the doctor; he throws away as much of his typology as he can and accepts this unforeseeable thing that goes on between therapist and patient. This change goes along with a "medical realism" which, unlike the ordinary use of the term, is no acceptance of general concepts but accepting this situation as it is in its uniqueness. Although I am not allowed to renounce either typology or method, I must know in what moment I must give them up.

DR. DAVID RIOCH: Could you differentiate giving up hypotheses for data from giving them up for the unique?

BUBER: People cannot communicate about objectified things except in a certain common language.

RIOCH: You have past experience, present experience, and formulation.

BUBER: Yes, but formulation is secondary.

RIOCH: Formulation is primary since you can't have a datum without formulation.

BUBER: Experience is the presupposition of all formulation. I mean the real meeting of therapist and patient which precedes formulae and data.

RIOCH: There is a distinction between hypotheses based on data and hypotheses based on inference, *e.g.*, the unconscious, hostility, and love. A lot of these derivations are being given up, and quite usefully.

BUBER: Yes, I don't contest it. But the main thing is what is different from other experiences and inferences and not what is common.

RIOCH: Do you know anyone who has had a night of lucidity without having worked diligently on a problem beforehand?

BUBER: Yes, myself—in general not, but once or twice as a surprise, with a character of continuous surprise, and it determined the course of my other thought afterward.

RIOCH: When you get something, is it necessary to check it?

BUBER: Never in the process itself, sometimes afterward. The sad thing is that I forget it.

3

FARBER: There seem to be three areas of implications of your theory of the unconscious: for Freudian theory, for the dialogic as compared to the psychological approach, and for therapy in general.

BUBER: I don't know about the implications of my ideas in various fields. When I am asked, I begin to think about them. I was about forty when I began to think about these things. I got the impression that different men in different fields became interested and wanted to transpose these ideas. I was willing to be used. In 1923 or so the psychotherapists began to be interested and wanted to talk with me. And I talked and talked. They, not I, made the implications. I will try tonight, but I have no conclusions or consequences. If you ask me a question, I will just begin to think about it.

FARBER: Since you say Freud made a mistake in making the unconscious psychic, what does your theory imply concerning Freud's bringing over the contents of the unconscious to consciousness—for repression, fixation, transference, and free association?

BUBER: Making the conscious unconscious means there are repressed elements which the patient did not want to keep. He put them down into Acheron, and now the therapist induces him to bring them out into the open. If the unconscious is not something psychic that can be preserved in the underground but just a piece of human body and soul existence, it cannot at all again be raised as it was. We do not have a deep freeze which keeps fragments, but this unconscious has its own existence which can again be dissociated into physical and psychic phenomena, but it can mean a radical change of the substance. This radical change can be brought up by the patient under the supervision, help, and even initiative of the therapist. This new dissociation can be brought up in very different ways, but every time a radical change is going on. What is the meaning of this curious cooperation between two persons in the course of which this change and elaboration is being made? Transference is a presupposition of this, but even the concept of transference changes radically if it is not to make the unconscious conscious but the elaboration of dissociated elements. This is a unique cooperation, the material of which is just a lump of the substance of the other. If the aim is to bring up something that is lying in the underground, then the therapist is only a kind of midwife. But if this work means real and sometimes radical change of the substance, then transference implies eminently a certain influence of the therapist on the very act being made. The patient has the impression of discovery going on in relation to something contained in his soul and in unconscious form. This is a mistake of the patient induced by the relation between him and the therapist. He brings up what he senses is wanted of him. I would ask the therapists of the world to examine anew the nature of this unique transference relationship.

MARGARET RIOCH: This puts great responsibility on the therapist.

BUBER: *Yes.* Since something is made and produced, rather than just being brought up. No other relationship produces such strange phenomena. The responsibility in this new concept is shared and is not only up to the therapist.

FARBER: Freud moved from hypnosis to free association. How would you describe free association?

BUBER: It is usually described as putting the patient in such an attitude that he does not direct his thoughts but lets himself say what comes to mind. My question is: is this indeed free association? What makes us think it is free?

FARBER: It is clear—we agree it is rare—the patient would not need our help if he could free associate.

BUBER: There are two kinds of therapists, one who knows more or less consciously the kind of interpretation he will get and the other, the psychologist who does not know. I am entirely on the side of the latter, who does not want something precise. He is ready to receive what he will receive. He cannot know what method he will use beforehand. He is, so to speak, in the hands of his patient. You cannot interpret different material by the same method. Take, for example, literary texts. You cannot interpret poetry by the same methods as a novel. In the world of patients the differences are greater than this. In the interpretation of dreams, if a therapist is not a Freudian, Jungian or Adlerian, but is what the man puts to him, he is a better therapist. There is more in common to literature than to people. The interpretation of dreams becomes more and more difficult without categories. He must be ready to be surprised. From this a new type of therapist may evolve—a person of greater responsibility and even greater gifts, since it is not so easy to master new attitude without ready-made categories. I see this new willingness to be surprised in the writings of Sullivan.* This has an analogy in the physical sciences where terminology is being changed. New terminology is needed to express Niels Bohr's theory of complementarities—the one I think most important of the theories of our day.

---

* Harry Stack Sullivan, author of *The Interpersonal Conception of Psychiatry* and leading spirit of the Washington School of Psychiatry —M.F.

EDITH WEIGERT: I understand about liberating ourselves from categories yet one needs some charted expectations. Is there not a middle way which will avoid preconceived ideas yet have some line of direction of expectation of what is to be found?

BUBER: The usual therapist imposes himself on the patient without being aware of it. What I mean is the conscious liberation of the patient from this unconscious imposition of the therapist—leaving the patient really to himself and seeing what comes out of it. The therapist approaches the patient, but he must try to influence him as little as possible, *i.e.,* the patient must not be influenced by the general ideas of the school. The patient must be left to himself, if I may say so, with the humility of the master, and then the therapist awaits the unexpected and does not put what comes into the categories. (Analogous to the interpretation of the poem.) It is much easier to impose than to use the whole force of the soul to leave him to himself and not to touch him, so to speak. When I read of an unknown poet, I cannot use any method when I receive this poem. If you judge Eliot by Keats you fail. The real master responds to uniqueness.

MAURICE FRIEDMAN: Is the unconscious, instead of a psychic sphere within, a sphere which has *more* direct contact with and part in the interhuman than the psychic? If so, would notions such as introjection and projection be partially open to question on this ground?

BUBER: This must be rethought, but it will take time— twenty years. The new therapist may not be called a psychologist or psychotherapist by that time. In certain crises of later childhood I feel that more decisive formation is going on than in infancy. Social and cosmic puberty is what I refer to, and not just to sexual puberty, for they may not occur. We need new terms and a new approach. If it will be done, it must be by new methods, by new insights. If the unconscious is that part of the existence of a person in which the realms of body and soul are not dissociated, then the relationship between two persons would mean the relationship between two nondivided existences. Thus the highest moment of relation would be what we call unconscious. But unconscious should have, may have, will have, more influence in the interhuman than the conscious. For example, in shaking hands, if there is real desire to be in touch, the contact is not bodily or psychic, but a unity of one and the other. The unconscious as such does not enter easily into action. I pronounce a word, you receive it—the unconscious has no such means at its disposition. The unconscious sometimes leads to a half-articulated exclamation which all the prepared words cannot, however. The voice becomes the direct instrument of the unconscious in this case.

DR. RYCOFF: The patient suffers infinitely more from preconceptions than the therapist (his defenses). Does openness on the part of the therapist lead him to drop these defenses?

BUBER: Are you sure this is the normal attitude of the patient? In the time of strongest transfer is there not the need of the patient to give himself up in his unconscious into the hands of the therapist so that contact may arise between them?

RYCOFF: He cannot do this. He suffers from repetition—uses the same devices time after time and does not see the new in the situation.

BUBER: One doctor kept a diary on such things, and a year later laughed at his diagnoses.

RYCOFF: You would put your emphasis on the *receptivity* of the therapist?

BUBER: Yes, but I am not sure receptivity is the right word. But the therapist must be willing—so that the patient trusts existentially.

FARBER: Does your theory imply that healing takes place through meeting rather than through insight and analysis?

BUBER: A certain very important kind of healing—existential healing—takes place thus, healing not just of a certain part of the patient, but of the very roots of the patient's being.

DR. NELKIN: What would you think of saying that healing leads to meeting? Patients use devices to prevent meeting, and this is called disease. But if these devices are abandoned, that meeting may occur?

BUBER: I'm doubtful about this. Do you mean that the *patient* is the cause of the meeting's not taking place? There are certain difficulties on the side of the patient and some, perhaps not less, on the side of the therapist. Not everyone is a therapist who thinks himself one even though he has studied and has the given abilities. Let us look at the kind of relation called trust—existential trust of a whole person to another. What we call in general life trust has a particular representation in the domain of healing, and so long as it is not there, this need to give up into the hands of the therapist what is repressed will not be realized. I know some therapists in Europe rather intimately that were gifted and knew a lot, masters of methods who realized it took a long time to overcome the patient's difficulties (but who did not have trust).

FRIEDMAN: Does your view of the unconscious and of therapy imply confirmation instead of observation and transference? Or do transference and confirmation complement or include each other?

BUBER: Let us divide this question in two. Confirmation in this context is too general a term. A certain kind of confirmation should be specified. Secondly, confirmation does not replace transference, but if meeting is the decisive factor, the other concepts would change also, in both their meaning and their dynamic. Everything is changed in real meeting. Confirmation can be misunderstood as *static*. I meet another —I accept and confirm him as he now is. But confirming a person *as he is* is only the first step, for confirmation does not mean that I take his appearance at this moment as the person I want to confirm. I must take the other person in his dynamic existence, in his specific potentiality. How can I confirm what I want most to confirm in his present being? That is the hidden, for in the present lies hidden what *can become.* His potentiality makes itself felt to me as that which I would most confirm. (In religious terms, his created purpose.)

FRIEDMAN: Is there a special kind of confirmation for therapy?

BUBER: I am inclined to think that in the strongest illness manifesting itself in the life of a person the highest potentiality of this person is manifesting itself in negative form.

X: In healing this illness, is the therapist confirming the negative?

BUBER: The therapist can influence in a direct way the growing up of potentialities. Healing is not the bringing up of the old, but of the new, not bringing up of zero, but counterbalancing with the positive.

WOLFGANG WEIGERT: Don't I dissociate every time I become aware of myself? What is dissociative experience?

BUBER: The unconscious is not a phenomenon, either physiological or psychic, and we never experience it directly but only know it by its effects, by the dissociation of the lump into body and soul phenomenon. Dissociation is the process of its manfesting itself in inner and outer perceptions.* The conscious life of the patient is a dualistic life, as he knows it; his objective life is not dualistic, but he doesn't know it.

W. WEIGERT: Is this dualism an illness?

BUBER: No, it is just the biography of body-soul. No man can know his own unity.

DAVID RIOCH: What can you say about God in healing?

BUBER: In that moment when the name of God is mentioned, most human circles break asunder as persons without knowing it. In that moment the commonness of thinking—the fact of thinking together—is disrupted. The difference between the world with God and without is so enormous that discussion of God must divide except in a group united by a

---

* This is perhaps the origin of our whole sense of "inner" and "outer"—M.F.

real common faith. People say God without meaning reality, as a sublime convention of a cultured person.

X: If man cannot know his own unity, does this mean that he can't know his self?

BUBER: To say man cannot perceive his unity as an object does not mean that he can have no conception of his self. In rare moments he may feel the uniting of his forces, each force in its own sphere, united without losing its own essence. This uniting is the precondition of real decisions. A decision made with only a part of a man is not true decision. Man can have in a certain measure the consciousness, the feeling of this coming together of his forces, his acting unity, but he cannot perceive his unity as an object. As long as man perceives the self as an object, he is not united.

DR. CAMERON: Can you enlarge on the nature of the shaping memory?

BUBER: The birth and growth of legends is a good example. Something occurs that is so overwhelming that those who experience it cease to be faithful chroniclers and in utter innocence remember it as a miracle. The memory shapes what occurred.

CAMERON: Are you aware in your dream that you are dreaming, shaping?

BUBER: You cannot remember a dream otherwise than by shaping it. Your inner action is a part of the result of what you call the content of the dream. There is an active part in dreams themselves as well that bears some analogy to action in waking life.

CAMERON: Does this relate to distance? This standing back appears in schizophrenia—"This is crazy."

BUBER: The schizophrenic has a "double memory." He dwells in a common world and in his own world. Example "Der Oberdada"* with his diary of Weimer (1910).

MARGARET RIOCH: Is there an essential difference between

---

* Founder of Dadaism—M.F.

the teacher-pupil relationship, on the one hand, and the therapist-patient relationship on the other?

BUBER: The two have in common the fact that teacher and therapist experience the relationship from the side of pupil and patient and not vice-versa. The teacher experiences from his side *and* from the pupil's, but there is no reciprocity there; the pupil cannot and should not experience the teacher's side. If he does, there is no teacher-pupil relation, but it breaks or they become friends. The same thing is true for the therapist and the patient. The therapist must feel the other side as a bodily touch to know how the patient feels it. If the patient could do this, there would be no need of therapy and no relationship. But there is an essential difference. There exists a specific, legitimate, rather problematic but nonetheless legitimate, superiority of the therapist. He cannot go on without it. He must, of course, be humble in it if he is to be a therapist. I don't think a teacher has a real superiority. The therapist in the most favorable cases can heal really. No teacher can teach perfectly. The teacher is a rather tragic person because in most cases learning is fragmentary.

RIOCH: The therapist is fragmentary too. There is no complete development of the person.

BUBER: The existential element means bringing the patient to self-healing, which is the same task as teaching.

POLITICS BORN OF FAITH

I WILL NOT speak of the political situation of
the Jews but of Jewish faith and what it has to say with regard to the public life of man.

The Jewish faith needs this people that it may live its faith.
The people shall be constituted through its faith. Only from
faith, from revelation does this nationality exist. Only through
receiving the word did it become a people. Its legitimate existence depends upon the condition of whether it is ready to
fulfill this faith with its whole life. But this people was not
given a faith that claimed only a part of man, not a faith
that only hovers above the waters. Rather precisely that is
the essential, that the faith not only may not content itself
with a sundering of life, but it wants, even in the beginning
at Sinai, to claim the *whole* life and must do so. This total
claim was already raised and recognized at that time when
the band gathered at the foot of the mountain communally
spoke the word of God. This faith announces itself in the
fact that even earlier, before they had come to the foot of
the mountain, just this band become people had proclaimed
the Lord of the Word their only king. King he remains in
time and eternity.

But this was not only the situation for a historical moment.
When now this people had received the Land of Promise,
their leaders sought to realize this proclamation of the one
king. They took this constitution of the king as seriously as
one could take it—politically seriously. They wanted to establish a community whose real ruler is the Lord. They
wanted to give God the honor. Gideon rejected for himself

and his descendants the hereditary kingship with the words:
"I will not rule over you, and my son also shall not rule over
you; the Lord shall rule over you." (Judges 8:23.) God also
has the title of king. Among all the peoples there existed only
within this people the conception of the rulership of God.
A constitution of the state in which God alone has the rights
of king, this real taking seriously the subjection to God—that
is the history of Israel. That it has dared that is the life justi-
fication of this people.*

Since then this people has gone on wrong and side paths,
but the unbowed will to that taking seriously has not been
extinguished in them. No other values shall be regarded as so
great that one betrays God for their sake. This God, who
even today still lives in the remnant part of the people, the
people also wants to serve, but in full free will. And for that
it does not matter whether one names God's name if only
one truly means the right. Faith is the victorious and trium-
phant message. That we have this faith, despite all our wrong
and side paths, enables us to hope.

Redemption means the completion of God's creation to
the kingdom of God. In spite of all obstacles we believe that
this way of God exists because it is his will. It is the redemption that will embrace the whole world. The thought of redemption cannot rest until the whole world, without deduction, enters into the kingdom of God. The irreducible in this
faith also has the meaning that man, despite all his errors,
shall have his share in the work of the completion of creation. *God needs man because he wills to need him.* God has
chosen him for this comradeship. This uncanny and necessary thought results in the connection of our faith with our
personal life. The kingdom of man and the community of
God coincide. A human community willed by man cannot

---

* Martin Buber has grounded this thesis with utmost scholarly
thoroughness in his book *Kingship of God,* trans. by Richard Schei-
mann. (New York: Harper and Row, 1967)—M.F.

yet be the kingdom of God. For it forms part of it that we join our willing of the human community with the community with God. What we can prepare can enter into this world of God's community of which we can have only a presentiment.

Because it is thus, for our faith the history of the world and of the human race is indeed real in faith, and, to be sure, the whole history without any deduction. Men certainly often tend to extract a part of history and then call it sacred history. But that means to regard this part as privileged and to detach it from history. Every such particularism, however, is the *wrong* way. Through the mouth of Amos, God spoke thus to his people: "Are you not to me like the people of Ethiopia, you children of Israel? Have I not led Israel out of the land of Egypt, and the Philistines out of Caphtor and the Syrians out of Kir?" (Amos 9:7) All these peoples are liberated by the one God, by whatever name they may call him. And in Isaiah 19:23-25, it says: "On that day a paved road will lead from Egypt to Assyria; the Assyrians will come to Egypt and the Egyptians to Assyria, and the Egyptians will worship the Lord with the Assyrians. On that day will Israel be a third in a covenant next to Egypt and Assyria, a blessing in the midst of the earth, whom the Lord of hosts blesses by saying: Blessed is Egypt, my people, and Assyria, the work of my hands, and Israel, my inheritance!" Hence these two great enemy world kingdoms, Assyria and Egypt, between which Canaan lay and which always regarded this land as a football, will be accepted by God at the end of days and put on a par with Israel. For all times and for all peoples it is thereby said that no "sacro egoismo" can and may exist. The whole of history, without deduction, is real in faith. Therefore nothing can exist in it that can lay the claim to holiness only for itself.

In Dostoevsky's *The Possessed,* Shatov says approximately the following: Each people has its God whom it addresses and expresses. The Gods of these peoples fight with one another—that is world history. That is the most extreme anti-thesis to what the prophets of Israel have said. Nationality there as here, but the question is what degree of sovereignty one accords the individual nation, whether the nation may deify itself or whether all peoples want to place themselves under the one rule. Israel is only summoned to its life in so far as it does not place itself under that spirit of the peoples which is independent in the face of God. To them, the Israel-ites, it is said: Do not believe that you are secure in your promises; what matters is how you answer God with your deeds. The election is bound to the fulfillment of the will of God. This responsibility drives out every false consciousness of sovereignty. The election is not a special prerogative *vis à vis* the other peoples, for they too are God's creatures. In the Talmud the significant legend is told: When the Egyptian troops were drowned by the waves while passing through the Red Sea, then the angels that stood around the throne of God wanted to sing a song of praise. But the Lord spoke to them: My creatures are sinking in the sea, and you want to rejoice?

Each hour into which we are placed is real in faith. For the human share is included in history. All these endlessly dispersed hours of man are melted down into what we call the historical decision. No man is excepted from the address of God. God speaks to each of us, and each is summoned to answer with his doing and not doing. This dialogue between God and man, God and world, is the historical hour.

There is no special law of God for the groups and no special law for the individuals. Man is bound in duty as an individual and as one who belongs to a group.

The faith of Israel in the redemption of the world does not signify that this world will be replaced by another; rather it is the faith in a new world *on this earth*. The here and the beyond does not exist in Hebrew. This hope including the whole world signifies that we cannot talk with God if we abandon the world to itself. We can only talk with God when we put our arms, as well as we can, around the world, that is when we carry God's truth and justice to all.

It is not valid to pursue a special "messianic" politics. But there is a certain manner of participation in public life by which in the midst of the interaction with world and politics the glance can be kept directed to the kingdom of God. There is no religious sanction for the setting of political aims. There is no political party that can assert that only it is willed by God. But it is also not so that one could say that before God it makes no difference whether this or that is done. From the standpoint of God's will it is not indifferent whether this or that happens; there are commands and prohibitions not only for the individuals but also for the community.

God gives each historical hour its sign, and what matters is that we men see this sign and answer it rightly. Thus it is clear today, for example, that community shall be something real and genuine. The property of an individual ought not to increase so much that genuine communal existence is disturbed. Therefore the right of God bids that such property be given up. A balancing must take place between those with property and those without. Or another example, if one man has become enslaved, then the balance must be created so that he again becomes free; for it is God's law that man be free. The law of Israel speaks ever again of the rights of the unprotected man. There ought not to be men outside the security of life. The significance of community in Israelite law is a dynamic and not a static one. But that holds for all peoples, for God is not only the God of Israel. There is no religious and social program, but there is this not-to-be-misunderstood indication of what is right and wrong in the society. There is no firmly established law, formulated once for all, but only the word of God and our current situation which we have to learn by listening. We do not have codified principles that we can consult. But we must understand the situation and the moment.

We must begin with the realization of God here where we

are placed. There is no realization unless we live from faith. Living from faith I may not will the realization of holy ends by unholy means. If I do not use holy means, then no holy way can exist. We may not separate religion and politics from each other. The real faith must take in everything. That is often fearfully difficult and many times a dangerous undertaking. But faith must acknowledge as its own the duty to penetrate politics in so far as it can. On this road one often has fearful experiences, but they cannot be spared one. Each in his responsibility in his life must approach realization by bowing before God and being sure that before this King all power of the world is unreal.

IN TWENTY YEARS

YOU ADDRESS to me the question: What do I think the world will be like in twenty years. I cannot answer this question even by way of conjecture. I presuppose, to be sure, even as you do, "that by the joint efforts of the nations war will be averted and mankind will be able to develop in peaceful conditions." But everything depends upon what the word peace signifies here: mere cessation of the cold war or real coexistence. But if the way is not to lead to a new and still more dangerous cold war such as may be expected from further technical development, real coexistence can and may mean nothing less than real cooperation for the mastery of the common problems of the human race that are growing ever more critical. Despite the fundamental difference of views of social justice and individual freedom, I hold such a cooperation, precisely in the sense of a genuine socialism, to be possible if in direct, unprejudiced, and comprehensive discussion qualified, independent, and realistically thinking men from both camps succeed in recognizing the urgency of vital common interests and drawing from it the practical consequences that it will yield for a cooperation. What is attained in these discussions and to what extent the leaders of the great camps will understand how to transpose what is attained into reality, upon that depends, along with other things, "man's motto in 1981" about which you ask.

ON TWO BURCKHARDT SAYINGS

To THE ASSERTION of the historian Jacob Burck-hardt, which has been taken up again and supplemented, that power is evil in itself, Carl Burckhardt rejoined in his Munich speech of 1960 that power can be everything, good and evil. This simple statement is exactly to the point. Power signifies, indeed, first of all the sheer ability to effect what one wants to effect, evil and good. But what is meant clearly goes beyond that. The great writer of history had indeed, certainly deliberately thrusting aside Plato's so-emphatic dis-tinction between Dionysios men and Dion-men, added, "No matter who wields it." He has thereby given us to understand that the possessor of power, under the influence of his having power, becomes evil, *i.e.,* naturally, not simply "an evil man," but one who wields evil power. Carl Burckhardt contests implicitly the general validity of this idea of the inner effects of power. And again, to get to the bottom of the matter, one must compare the text of *Reflections on History.** "It is no persevering," it says there, "but an inordinate desire." It is this necessarily fateful coupling of power with the will to power that our contemporary, thinking both as a statesman and as a historian, contests. Only when the will to power reaches beyond the current potential of the possessor of power to master the situation historically demanding him does he fall to evil.

---

* Jacob Burckhardt, *Force and Freedom: Reflections on History,* translated with an Introduction by James Hastings Nichols (New York: Meridian Books, 1955)—M.F.

The distinction between good and evil rightly continues in existence beyond Nietzsche's great rebellion against the assertion of Jacob Burckhardt of which he learned in 1870. But what has happened since then has taught us to make this distinction more sharply, more exactly, more in accordance with the history that is happening.

A CONVERSATION WITH TAGORE

IT IS about twenty-five years since Rabindranath Tagore invited me to meet with him to discuss the problem of Zionism and the Jewish settlement of Palestine. The meeting took place in Prague at the home of the Sanskrit professor Winternitz.

I did not note down the course of the talk, but I can sketch its essential content from memory.

Tagore expressed his fear that a return of the Jewish people to national independence would have an unfavorable effect on its character. It would weaken its finest characteristic, the one most valuable for mankind, which he described as reverence for the spirit and universalism. While it was in dispersion among the peoples, however much endangered by their influences, it was protected from these by its special nature inherited from its early times. Grown to self-determination, it would now become assimilated as a people to the narrow-hearted nationalism and soulless pantechnicism of the Western nations in order to be able to hold its own on this most difficult geopolitical point, Palestine.

I answered that the danger indicated did, in fact, exist, but it would not do to evade it. As in the life of individuals, so in that of peoples, there exist in a certain stage of their way threatening dangers necessary for life, so to speak, which one must attack directly in order eventually to overcome them. If in the pressing historical hour one flees from them, one loses the capacity for advancing further, becomes paralyzed, and expires. What is important is to direct one's best forces to the meeting with the danger: for then it will either evaporate or we must fight and conquer it with our concentrated forces.

In the case of the Jewish people in this hour that signifies two kinds of things: internally, to fill Zionism itself with that inherited treasure, reverence for the spirit and universalism, and thus to install the antidote within it; externally, however, to accomplish the work of settlement in Palestine in agreement with the peoples of the Orient, yes in union with them, in order together with them to erect a great federative structure which could learn and receive from the West those positive ends and means that are to be learned and received from it, without succumbing to the influences of its inner disorder and goallessness.

Tagore nodded assent but protested that the civilization of the West, despite the manifestations of degeneration in it, is too powerful for one to be able thus at the same time both to accept it and protect oneself from it. One must oppose to its machines and canons the principle of being of the East, genuine meditation; one must demonstrate to the Occident the emptiness and meaninglessness of its bustle and teach it, together with the Orient, to plunge into the vision of the eternal truth.

I contested this. He should imagine, I said, a man who carried up a mountain a heavy sign in order to plant it at the summit. Someone comes upon him halfway up, shakes his head over his senseless intention and advises him to cast off the heavy load, then his ascent would be easy. "Not so," the man answers, "I climb upward, in fact, just in order to erect this sign up above. I hold it, and it holds me." This is the situation, despite all, of the human spirit today. It may not cast off the burden of its civilization; for in it a higher value is hidden that will only shine forth when from the sphere of inner conflict it attains the pure summit air of justice and peace.

"And the Jews?" asked Tagore.

"The Jews," I replied, "are the most exposed point of

modern mankind. The venture and chance of civilization becomes concentrated in their existence; their existence itself is an experiment. That will only be still further intensified in Palestine. We must attack the danger directly in order to overcome it. To do this we need your brotherly help."

Tagore extended his hand to me, and what I felt he surely felt, too—that in the midst of all the hazards of the history of the nations there is a fact of facts which endures uninjured —human brotherliness.

CHINA AND US

IT HAPPENS from time to time that a call comes to Europe from the East to make common cause with Asia. I recall a remark of Tagore's. He said, approximately, "Indeed, why do you do all this here in Europe? Why do you have all this bustle, all this industrialization, all this ballast? All of this is really quite unnecessary. Cast off all this and let us, West and East, contemplate truth in common." That was said in a heartfelt manner. But it seemed to me removed from the reality of the hour in which we live. I pictured to myself a man who proposed to erect a great symbol on a mountain peak that had not yet been conquered and who climbed up the mountain burdened with this symbol. If someone should now call to him, "Why all the trouble? Just throw away that heavy thing, then you will ascend much more easily!" then the man would rightly answer, "I intend either to ascend with this symbol or to fall headlong with it."

It is this burden that the West is called upon to master. Upon the real mastering of it depends whether this epoch will fulfill its meaning or not. Stripping off the burden and going back behind all this industrializing and technicizing and mechanizing, we would no longer proceed on the way at all; we would, in general, no longer have a way. It is not so, therefore, that we could give up all of this in order now, together with the Oriental, to seek and contemplate what is common to both. Rather we can only come together with them, taking with us this our task, with its problematic, its element of disintegration, which we experience today and of which we can reduce nothing. We must take it upon us as it is, bear it as it is, overcome it as it is. If we pass through our task thus, then we may hope to meet an Asia advancing to meet us. May it be spared our road! But when I consider the development of Japan—yes, even the development of India —I doubt whether it can be spared it.

But within this problematic, can the contact with Asia nonetheless have some significance for us? Do we still have something to take, to receive, from Asia? Understand me rightly, not in the intellectual manner that was customary in the eighteenth century, when one superficially appropriated any sort of external product of Chinese art or wisdom. Not, for example, in the way in which the secret of the Chinese art of engraving was elaborated into the in-part-very-charm-ing *chinoiserie*. Nor in the way in which one took hold of Confucian wisdom, not according to its concrete original contents, but only just as something universally noble and valuable, without perceiving that such receiving is a sin against the spirit, that real receiving can only take place as the receiving of a living reality with the forces of one's own life. I do not mean this. But the question is, is there some-thing that we can receive from living Chinese reality, from the real life powers of its customs, its education, its culture, and if so what?

It does not seem to me now that there is anything that we can take over in this sense from the Confucian culture.

I shall advance only two of the reasons for my view. One concerns the most important foundation of this culture: its ancestor cult. That is, of course, a concept by which one usually understands things of very different natures. An an-cestor cult exists among the so-called primitives, from dread before the continuing, horrifying, sinister presence of the dead, whom one wishes to propitiate. Another ancestor cult exists in which the ancestors migrate into a higher sphere of existence, becoming demons, heroes, gods—detached from, and incapable of being touched by, the vicissitudes of earthly life. They are, thereby, only an object of veneration for the later human generations, but not a living relationship. The Chinese ancestor cult is of an entirely different nature. It signifies an attitude of the receiving principle; it means that the generation that lives after receives from the dead. This ancestor cult is thus only possible in a culture where familiarity with the dead prevails. I mean familiarity, therefore neither horror nor distant veneration, but natural intercourse without any uncanniness, such as the Chinese tales again and again tell us of, most clearly in the stories of love relationships with the dead. Here is nothing of the horror of the medieval incubus; one has intercourse, as on the same plane, with the spirits of the dead who have entered into our life. This case of intercourse with the dead goes together with the Chinese type of ancestor cult. The generation that lives after receives from the generation that we call the past. And thereby the seed of the custom, the formation is ever again planted in the growing generation—not as something that is only held fast, only continued, only preserved, but as something that engenders and whose engendering is reborn in the new generation, seemingly this same custom and yet formed anew, grown anew.

That is something that must certainly remain alien to the West. The foundations of this ancestor cult are not given in the West. An organic relation between the dead and the living, as in the Chinese culture, is not present in the West, and is, it seems to me, not possible. And that is one reason why I doubt that such a connection of the generations, such a belief of the new in the old that is for it precisely *not* the old, could grow here. It might certainly be necessary for us; for we have entered into a crisis not merely of the individual institutions, but of our institutions in general. But I do not see how we could take over what offers itself here.

The second reason is that culture is always connected with an image and, in fact, with a universally valid image. There exists, indeed, not merely universally valid concepts, as philosophy teaches, but also universally valid images. The ages that possess real culture are ages where a universally valid image of man stands above the heads of men. Looking upward to these images that are invisible and yet living in the imagination of all individuals constitutes the life of culture; the imitation of them out of the material of the person is the educating, the forming of man. Now, however, the East Asian image is a different species from that of the Occident. The universally valid image of man in China is the original man, the "pure man of yore." Erected on the ancestor cult of China, this image is a monument of the trust in the original state, in that which must ever again be reborn, ever again formed anew. This trust in the primal being is missing in the Western man and cannot be acquired by him. Even Christianity was not able to alter this situation, although it did, in fact, transmit to the West the Oriental teaching of the paradisiacal primal state of mankind. Of the biblical story of the first man, only the fall is present in a living way in the reality of the personal life of Christian Western man, not the life before the fall. The trust in the original being of the human substance is lacking, and I do not believe that it is to be won on the paths of the historical culture visible to us. (You understand that I do not speak of other paths. We speak of the relations of cultures to each other; we speak of the historical, not of the superhistorical that may ever again burst through and transform the historical.) These are two of the reasons that make me doubt whether we can absorb into our life something of the great connection of China, its continuity, something of that warranting of the institutional principle that the Chinese culture offers.

But there is still something that we can receive and actually from the standpoint of the progress of our history, of our experiences in this world hour. That is not, to be sure, something of the great structure of the Confucian culture; it is something revolutionary, protestant, though basically, of course, ancient. I believe that we can receive from China in a living manner something of the Taoist teaching of "nonaction," the teaching of Lao-tzu. And for the reason that—bearing our burden on our way—we have learned something analogous, only negatively—on the reverse side, so to speak. We have begun to learn, namely, that success is of no consequence. We have begun to doubt the significance of historical success, *i.e.,* the validity of the man who sets an end for himself, carries this end into effect, accumulates the necessary means of power and succeeds with these means of power: the typical modern Western man. I say, we begin to doubt the content of existence of this man. And there we come into contact with something genuine and deeply Chinese, though not, to be sure, Confucian: with the teaching that genuine effecting is not interfering, not giving vent to power, but remaining within one's self. This is the powerful existence that does not yield historical success, *i.e.,* the success that can be exploited and registered in this hour, but only yields that effecting that at first appears insignificant, indeed invisible, yet endures across generations and there at times becomes perceptible in another form. At the core of each historical process hides the turning away from what the man who accomplished it really had in mind. Not realization, but the hidden nonrealization that has been disguised or masked just through success is the essence of historical success. Opposed to it stands the changing of men that takes place in the absence of success, the changing of men through the fact that one effects without interfering. It is, I believe, in the commencing knowledge of this action without doing, action through nonaction, of this powerfulness of existence, that we can have contact with the great wisdom of China. With us this knowledge does not originate as wisdom but as foolishness. We have obtained a taste of it in the bitterest manner; indeed, in a downright foolish manner. But there where we stand or there where we shall soon stand, we shall directly touch upon the reality for which Lao-tzu spoke.

ON "CIVIL DISOBEDIENCE"

IT IS NOW nearly sixty years since I became acquainted with Henry Thoreau's tract on "Civil Disobedience." I read it with the strong feeling: this is something that directly concerns me. But only very much later did I understand from where that feeling came. It was the concrete, the personal, the "here and now" in the writing that won my heart for it. Thoreau did not formulate a general principle as such; he set forth and grounded his attitude in a particular historical-biographical situation. He spoke to his reader in the realm of this situation common to them so that the reader not only learned why Thoreau at that time acted as he acted, but also—provided that this reader was only honest and unbiased—that he himself, the reader, must have acted, should the occasion present itself, in just such a way if he was seriously concerned about making his human existence real.

It is not simply a question here of one of the many individual cases of the struggle of a powerless truth against a power that has become inimical to truth. It is a question of the wholly concrete indication of the point at which time and again this struggle becomes the duty of man *as man*. Because from his historical situation Thoreau speaks as concretely as he does, he expresses in the right manner what is valid for all human history.

MORE ON "CIVIL DISOBEDIENCE"

I AM ever again asked wherein—not in a particular historical situation, but wholly in general—civil disobedience can prove its legitimacy. To this I know, first of all, nothing else to answer than: Disobedience of such a nature is only legitimate if it is in truth obedience, more exactly, obedience to a higher authority than the one that one here and now obeys. But now I shall be met with a new question: From where then do I know the command of this highest authority for this situation here and now? One can perhaps transpose this question into the language of the Gospel parable: "Where is the limit of that which I must at any time give to Caesar?"

Every attempt to answer this question unassailably from the plane of a generally valid concept must end in failure. The Absolute cannot show itself in our world as unconditionally superior to everything relative because the mighty-voiced apes of the Absolute understand how, with the requisite dialectical means, to demonstrate effectively their claims, each his own, in order to stigmatize the disobedient.*

Every Caesar, every Caesarism, no matter in what form it appears, every historically consistent power, poses to its subjects as existing through the grace of God, no matter what name this God may bear.

It is, therefore, finally necessary again for us to put an end to questioning and answering in general concepts and to make

---

* For a significantly related use of the phrase "the apes of the Absolute," see Buber, *Eclipse of God,* "On the Suspension of the Ethical," trans. by Maurice Friedman, pp. 115-120.

192

it unmistakably clear that, questioning and answering, one must keep the situation continually in sight. Not where at all times and in all places my obedient disobedience legitimately begins is what I have to say, but where it begins here and now.

Yet in the situation in which we live this has become easier to say than in any earlier situation of the human race.

For man through his own action is on the point of letting the determination of his fate slip out of his hands. Those who today make all-embracing preparations deny themselves the image of what possibility opens up through just these preparations. It is the possibility that in the course of the mutually outstripping bellicose surprises on the side of both partners, so to speak—with the seeming continuation of human institutions—the most dangerous of our powers will autonomously continue the game until it succeeds in transforming the human cosmos into a chaos beyond which we can no longer think.

Can the rulers of the hour command a halt to the machinery which they only seemingly master? Will they still be able at the right time to avert the pantechnical war? In other words, instead of the usual "political" talking *past* one another about mighty fictions, will they learn to talk *to* one another about the reality? Will they be able to clarify with one another the real mutual interests, to compare those that are opposed and those that are in common, and from this comparison to draw the conclusions that today every independent thinking person is already able to draw? But if, as I think, the rulers of the hour cannot do this, who shall come to the rescue here while there is still time if not the "disobedient," those who personally set their faces against the power that has gone astray as such? Must not a planetary front of such civil disobedients stand ready, not for battle like other fronts, but for saving dialogue? But who are these if not those who hear the voice that addresses them from the situation—the situation of the human crisis—and obey it?

ON CAPITAL PUNISHMENT

I CAN sum up my answer to the question placed before me in the following sentences: 1. Capital punishment is partially suicide without a legitimate subject. 2. It does not work as a deterrent, but through its terror it drives men still more deeply into the confusion. 3. Limits must be set to the self-protection of society through its aims, and they must be re-examined ever anew.

GENUINE DIALOGUE AND
THE POSSIBILITIES OF PEACE

I CANNOT express my thanks to the German Book Trade for the honor conferred on me without at the same time setting forth the sense in which I have accepted it, just as I earlier accepted the Hanseatic Goethe Prize given me by the University of Hamburg.

About a decade ago a considerable number of Germans—there must have been many thousands of them—under the indirect command of the German government and the direct command of its representatives, killed millions of my people in a systematically prepared and executed procedure whose organized cruelty cannot be compared with any previous historical event. I, who am one of those who remained alive, have only in a formal sense a common humanity with those who took part in this action. They have so radically removed themselves from the human sphere, so transposed themselves into a sphere of monstrous inhumanity inaccessible to my conception, that not even hatred, much less an overcoming of hatred, was able to arise in me. And what am I that I could here presume to "forgive"!

With the German people it is otherwise. From my youth on I have taken the real existence of peoples most seriously. But I have never, in the face of any historical moment, past or present, allowed the concrete multiplicity existing at that moment within a people—the concrete inner dialectic, rising to contradiction—to be obscured by the leveling concept of a totality constituted and acting in just such a way and no other.

When I think of the German people of the days of Au-

195

schwitz and Treblinka, I behold, first of all, the great many
who knew that the monstrous event was taking place and did
not oppose it. But my heart, which is acquainted with the
weakness of men, refuses to condemn my neighbor for not
prevailing upon himself to become a martyr. Next there
emerges before me the mass of those who remained ignorant
of what was withheld from the German public and who did
not try to discover what reality lay behind the rumors which
were circulating. When I have these men in mind, I am
gripped by the thought of the anxiety, likewise well known to
me, of the human creature before a truth which he fears he
cannot face. But finally there appear before me, from reliable
reports, some who have become as familiar to me by sight,
action, and voice as if they were friends, those who refused to
carry out the orders and suffered death or put themselves to
death, and those who learned what was taking place and
opposed it and were put to death, or those who learned what
was taking place and because they could do nothing to stop
it killed themselves. I see these men very near before me in
that especial intimacy which binds us at times to the dead and
to them alone. Reverence and love for these Germans now
fills my heart.

But I must step out of memory into the present. Here I am
surrounded by the youth who have grown up since those
events and had no part in the great crime. These youth, who
are probably the essential life of the German people today,
show themselves to me in a powerful inner dialectic. Their
core is included in the core of an inner struggle running for
the most part underground and only occasionally coming to
the surface. This is only a part, though one of the clearest, of
the great inner struggle of all peoples being fought out today,
more or less consciously, more or less passionately, in the
vital center of each people.

The preparation for the final battle of *homo humanus*
against *homo contrahumanus* has begun in the depths. But
the front is split into as many individual fronts as there are

peoples, and those who stand on one of the individual fronts know little or nothing of the other fronts. Darkness still covers the struggle, upon whose course and outcome it depends whether, despite all, a true humanity can issue from the race of men. The so-called cold war between two gigantic groups of states with all its accompaniments still obscures the true obligation and solidarity of combat, whose line cuts right through all states and peoples, however they name their régimes. The recognition of the deeper reality, of the true need and the true danger, is growing. In Germany, and especially in German youth, despite their being rent asunder, I have found more awareness of it than elsewhere. The memory of the twelve-year reign of *homo contrahumanus* has made the spirit stronger, and the task set by the spirit clearer, than they formerly were.

Tokens such as the bestowal of the Hanseatic Goethe Prize and the Peace Prize of the German Book Trade on a surviving arch-Jew must be understood in this connection. They, too, are moments in the struggle of the human spirit against the demonry of the subhuman and the antihuman. The survivor who is the object of such honors is taken up into the high duty of solidarity that extends across the fronts: the solidarity of all separate groups in the flaming battle for the rise of a true humanity. This duty is, in the present hour, the highest duty on earth. The Jew chosen as symbol must obey this call of duty even there, indeed, precisely there where the never-to-be-effaced memory of what has happened stands in opposition to it. When he recently expressed his gratitude to the spirit of Goethe, victoriously disseminated throughout the world, and when he now expresses his gratitude to the spirit of peace, which now as so often before speaks to the world in books of the German tongue, his thanks signify his confession of solidarity with the common battle—common also to Germans and Jews—against the contrahuman, and his reply to a vow taken by fighters, a vow he has heard.

Hearkening to the human voice, where it speaks forth un-falsified, and replying to it, this above all is needed today. The busy noise of the hour must no longer drown out the *vox humana,* the essence of the human which has become a voice. This voice must not only be listened to, it must be answered and led out of the lonely monologue into the awak-ening dialogue of the peoples. Peoples must engage in talk with one another through their truly human men if the great peace is to appear and the devastated life of the earth renew itself.

The great peace is something essentially different from the absence of war.

In an early mural in the town hall of Sienna the civic vir-tues are assembled. Worthy, and conscious of their worth, the women sit there, except one in their midst who towers above the rest. This woman is marked not by dignity but rather by composed majesty. Three letters announce her name: Pax. She represents the great peace I have in mind. This peace does not signify that what men call war no longer exists now that it holds sway—that means too little to enable one to understand this serenity. Something new exists, now really exists, greater and mightier than war, greater and mightier even than war. Human passions flow into war as the waters into the sea, and war disposes of them as it likes. But these passions must enter into the great peace as ore into the fire that melts and transforms it. Peoples will then build with one another with more powerful zeal than they have ever destroyed one another.

The Siennese painter had glimpsed this majestic peace in his dream alone. He did not acquire the vision from historical reality, for it has never appeared there. What in history has been called peace has never, in fact, been aught other than an anxious or an illusory blissful pause between wars. But the womanly genius of the painter's dream is no mistress of interruptions but the queen of new and greater deeds.

May we, then, cherish the hope that the countenance which

has remained unknown to all previous history will shine forth on our late generation, apparently sunk irretrievably in disaster? Are we not accustomed to describe the world situation in which we have lived since the end of the Second World War no longer even as peace but as the "cold" phase of a world war declared in permanence? In a situation which no longer even seeks to preserve the appearance of peace, is it not illusory enthusiasm to speak of a great peace which has never existed as being within reach?

It is the depth of our crisis that allows us to hope in this way. Ours is not a historically familiar malady in the life of peoples which can eventuate in a comfortable recovery. Primal forces are now being summoned to take an active part in an unrepeatable decision between extinction and rebirth. War has not produced this crisis; it is, rather, the crisis of man which has brought forth the total war, and the unreal peace which followed.

War has always had an adversary who hardly ever comes forward as such but does his work in the stillness. This adversary is speech, fulfilled speech, the speech of genuine conversation in which men understand one another and come to a mutual understanding. Already in primitive warfare fighting begins where speech has ceased; that is, where men are no longer able to discuss with one another the subjects under dispute or submit them to mediation, but flee from speech with one another and in the speechlessness of slaughter seek what they suppose to be a decision, a judgment of God. War soon conquers speech and enslaves it in the service of its battle cries. But where speech, be it ever so shy, moves from camp to camp, war is already called in question. Its cannons easily drown out the word; but when the word has become entirely soundless, and on this side and on that soundlessly bears into the hearts of men the intelligence that no human conflict can really be resolved through killing, not even through mass killing, then the human word has already begun to silence the cannonade.

But it is just the relation of man to speech and to dialogue that the crisis characteristic of our age has in particular tended to shatter. The man in crisis will no longer entrust his cause to dialogue because its presupposition—trust—is lacking. This is the reason why the cold war which today goes by the name of peace has been able to overcome mankind. In every earlier period of peace the living word has passed between man and man, time after time drawing the poison from the antagonism of interests and convictions so that these antagonisms have not degenerated into the absurdity of "no-farther," into the madness of "must-wage-war." This living word of human dialogue that from time to time makes its flights until the madness smothers it, now seems to have become lifeless in the midst of the nonwar. The debates between statesmen which the radio conveys to us no longer have anything in common with a human dialogue: the diplomats do not address one another but the faceless public. Even the congresses and conferences which convene in the name of mutual understanding lack the substance which alone can elevate the deliberations to genuine talk: candor and directness in address and answer. What is concentrated there is only the universal condition in which men are no longer willing or no longer able to speak directly to their fellows. They are not able to speak directly because they no longer trust one another, and everybody knows that the other no longer trusts him. If anyone in the hubbub of contradictory talk happens to pause and take stock, he discovers that in his relations to others hardly anything persists that deserves to be called trust.

And yet this must be said again and again, it is just the depth of the crisis that empowers us to hope. Let us dare to grasp the situation with that great realism that surveys all the definable realities of public life, of which, indeed, public life appears to be composed, but is also aware of what is most real of all, albeit moving secretly in the depths—the latent healing and salvation in the face of impending ruin. The power of turning that radically changes the situation never reveals itself outside of crisis. This power begins to function when one, gripped by despair, instead of allowing himself to be submerged calls forth his primal powers and accomplishes with them the turning of his very existence. It happens in this way both in the life of the person and in that of the race. In its depths the crisis demands naked decision: no mere fluctuation between the decomposition and the renewal of the tissue.

The crisis of man which has become apparent in our day announces itself most clearly as a crisis of trust, if we may employ, thus intensified, a concept of economics. You ask, trust in whom? But the question already contains a limitation not admissible here. It is simply trust that is increasingly lost to men of our time. And the crisis of speech is bound up with this loss of trust in the closest possible fashion, for I can only speak to someone in the true sense of the term if I expect him to accept my word as genuine. Therefore, the fact that it is so difficult for present-day man to pray (note well: not to hold it to be true that there is a God but to address Him) and the fact that it is so difficult for him to carry on a genuine talk with his fellow men are elements of a single set of facts. This lack of trust in Being, this incapacity for unreserved intercourse with the other, points to an innermost sickness of the sense of existence. One symptom of this sickness, and the most acute of all, is the one from which I have begun: that a genuine word cannot arise between the camps.

Can such an illness be healed? I believe it can be. And it is out of this, my belief, that I speak to you. I have no proof for this belief. No belief can be proved; otherwise it would not be what it is, a great venture. Instead of offering proof, I appeal to that potential belief of each of my hearers which enables him to believe.

If there be a cure, where can the healing action start? Where must that existential turning begin which the healing powers, the powers of salvation in the ground of the crisis, await?

That peoples can no longer carry on authentic dialogue with one another is not only the most acute symptom of the pathology of our time, it is also that which most urgently makes a demand of us. I believe, despite all, that the peoples in this hour can enter into dialogue, into a genuine dialogue with one another. In a genuine dialogue each of the partners, even when he stands in opposition to the other, heeds, affirms, and confirms his opponent as an existing other. Only so can conflict certainly not be eliminated from the world but be humanly arbitrated and led toward its overcoming.

To the task of initiating this conversation those are inevitably called who carry on today within each people the battle against the antihuman. Those who build the great unknown front across mankind shall make it known by speaking unreservedly with one another, not overlooking what divides them but determined to bear this division in common.

In opposition to them stands the element that profits from the divisions between the peoples, the contrahuman in men, the subhuman, the enemy of man's will to become a true humanity.

The name Satan means in Hebrew the hinderer. That is the correct designation for the antihuman in individuals and in the human race. Let us not allow this Satanic element in men to hinder us from realizing man! Let us release speech from its ban! Let us dare, despite all, to trust!

STOP!

IT IS NOW high time for men to tell the politicians: "We do not want mankind to embark upon annihilating itself. We do not want you to proceed with gambling, the stake of which is the life of the human race, and in which both partners must lose.

"We have given you the power you hold because we believed you to be persons who under any circumstances know what they do. We see we have been mistaken. The frenzy of the game has deprived you of the capacity to know the true nature of the game you play and whither it may lead. You are familiar with all the tricks and perform them methodically, but you are not aware that under your hands the game has changed into another one.

"Now the game is being played with you. You do not understand that if you will not stop now, a moment must come, and perhaps very soon, when the further course of events will not any more depend on you, and it will not any more be possible to stop. We know this process from former experiences, but the fiercest of them all is child's play compared with what will come this time if it comes. This time the war game will mean destruction of all the lands and peoples involved, till there remains nothing to be destroyed—and nobody to do the destruction.

"The basic law of the game says that the chance must not be less than the risk. Now the risk will be infinite and the chance nil. Desist, whilst it is yet possible to desist!"

And if they ask, what is the actual meaning of "to desist," the answer should be: "Always and everywhere there are conflicting interests, and people are fighting about them. But there is at times a limit, when the fight becomes absurd and compromise the only reasonable way. No so-called concilia-tion is meant, but a well-pondered compromise that can be justified before the generations to come and an adjustment of interests providing for the real vital needs of the peoples on both sides, after the well-considered deduction of those that are not vital. The limit has been reached. What do you your-selves prefer? Mutual concessions on the basis of discernment and fairness, or the unwilled suicide of mankind?"

ON THE ETHICS
OF POLITICAL DECISION

By "POLITICAL DECISION" one understands to-
day in general joining a political group. If this is done, then
all is finally in order; the time of political decision is past.
From now on, one need do nothing else than join in the
movements of the group to which one belongs. Never again
does one stand at a crossroads, never again does one have to
choose among the possible actions the right one; it is decided.
What one believed once, that ever anew, situation after situation, one has to be responsible for what is chosen at that
time, one is now rid of. The group has taken from one his
political responsibility. In it one feels oneself answered for;
one may feel so.

The attitude just indicated means, when it befalls a man of
faith (I will only speak of him here), his plunge from faith
—without his being inclined to confess, to admit it to himself
—his factual plunge from faith, no matter how loudly and
emphatically he himself continues to profess, shouting down
the innermost reality not merely with his mouth but also with
his soul.

One word of explanation beforehand, by man "of faith" I
understand no one other than he who has vowed himself to
the One Existing, God; to believe is to vow. One speaks readily in our time, certainly, of belief in a cause, in a people, in
a kingdom, yes in a party; but those are metaphors, useful
where one remains aware of their restriction, limitation, but
otherwise belonging to the representation of a modern pan-
theon in which the Baals of "causes" are enthroned, among
which each of us selects for himself the one he gets on with

well in order from then on to fight for it against the others. Genuine faith means genuine personal reciprocity; genuine faith exists only as relation of faith in which he to whom I have vowed myself himself holds and cherishes me. One also readily declares today that one believes "in the leader [*Füh-rer*]"; but the idols with human bodies are still worse than those in the form of ideas because they can counterfeit reality more effectively. The genuine leader who lets himself be led from above does not demand that one believe in him but that one, just for that reason, trust him—as Jesus rejected those who "believe in his name" on account of his "signs" (John 2:23ff.).

But the relationship of faith to the One Existing is perverted into appearance and self-deception if it is not exclusive. "Religion" may come to be understood as one division of life next to others, even as standing on its own and having its own law—it has thereby already perverted the relation of faith. To withdraw any realm basically from this its determining power means to want to withdraw from the determining power of God which rules over the relation of faith. To prescribe to the relation of faith, "You may determine so far what I have to do and no farther; at this boundary your power ends and that of the group to which I belong begins," means to speak just so to God. He who does not allow his relation of faith, as much as he can at any time, to be fulfilled in the unreduced measures of his lived life, has presumed to abridge God's rule over the world in its fullness.

The relation of faith is certainly no book of rules which one can consult to find what is to be done in this hour. What God demands of me in this hour, I learn, in so far as I learn it, not before but in it. But then too it is not given to me to learn it otherwise than when I am answerable before him, God, for it, this hour, as *my* hour, when I carry out responsibility for it toward him as much as I even now can. What has stepped up to me now, the unforeseen, the unforeseeable, is word from him, a word that stands in no dictionary, a word that now has become word—and what it demands of me is answer, my answer to it. I word my answer by choosing among the possible actions what appears to my devoted insight as the right one, by deciding myself for it. With my choice, my decision, my action—doing or leaving undone, intervening or forbearing—I answer the word, no matter how inadequately nonetheless legitimately; I answer for my hour. This responsibility my group cannot take from me; I may not let it take it from me. Otherwise I pervert my relation of faith; otherwise I neatly divide the sphere of my group from God's sphere of power.

Not as though nothing of my group concerned me in my decision; it concerns me enormously; by deciding I do not look away from the world, I look at it and in it. In it first of all, as what I must do justice to by my decision, I may see my group, on the welfare of which I depend. To it, before all, I may have to do justice. This, however, not for itself but for it in God's sight; and no program, no tactical resolution, no command of a leader can say to me how I, making my decision, must do justice to my group in God's sight. It can be that I may serve it in the way that program, resolution, command have ordered. It can mean that I shall serve it otherwise. It can even be—if in my act of decision such an unheard-of thing occurs to me—that I shall mercilessly oppose the success of its program because I have become aware that God loves it otherwise than for this success. What matters is only this: that I open my ear to the situation as it presents itself to me as to the word directed to me unto the ground where hearing flows into being, and hear what is to be heard, and answer what is heard. He who prompts me with an answer in such a way that he hinders me from hearing is the devil, whatever else he may be.

In no way is it meant that man must alone, without counsel, fetch the answer from his breast. Nothing of the kind is meant: how should the wisdom of the leaders, for example, not enter essentially into the substance from which the decision is cast? But it may not replace this decision; no substitute [*Ersatz*] is acceptable. He who trusts a leader may entrust himself to him, his bodily person but not his responsibility. He must open himself to his responsibility, equipped with all the oughts forged in the group, but exposed to the fate that in the abysmal moment all armor will fall away from him. He may even hold fast to the "interest" of the group with all his strength—until perhaps in the final confrontation with reality an exceedingly light, yet unmistakable finger touches on it. That is not, of course, the "finger of God," which we are not able to endure, and thus not the least certainty other than that of the personal rectitude of decision is admissible. God presents me with the situation which I must answer; that he presents me with anything of my answer I must not expect. Certainly in answering I am in the hands of his grace; but I cannot measure the share of what comes from above, and even the most blessed feeling of grace can deceive. The finger of which I speak is simply that of the "conscience," but not the customary, the useful conscience, used and used up, not the play of the surface with whose discrediting one presumed to have abolished the factuality of a positive answer of man. I point to the unknown conscience in the ground of being, which needs to be discovered ever anew, the conscience of the "spark," for a genuine spark is also operative in the united composure of each genuine decision.* The cer-

---

* Ronald Gregor Smith suggests in a note to his translation of the section of "The Question to the Single One" of which this essay was clearly an earlier draft that "the sparks" refer here to the teaching of Meister Eckhart, the great German mystic. (*Between Man and Man,* p. 69 and p. 208, note 13.) Despite Eckhart's great and lasting influence on Buber's thought, it seems equally likely to me that Buber is referring to the Hasidic teaching of the divine sparks that have descended into all things and are liberated by our actions when performed with *kavana,* inner intention or dedication. (See Martin Buber, *The Origin and Meaning of Hasidism,* ed. and trans. with an Introduction by Maurice Friedman (New York: Harper Torchbooks, 1966), pp. 54-56, 78-80, 84 ff. This would seem to be all the more so since Smith himself writes, "It is to be noted, however, that in Buber

tainty that this conscience engenders is, of course, only a personal one; it is an uncertain certainty; but what is *here* meant by person is just this person who is summoned and who answers.

I say, therefore, that the Single One, *i.e.,* the man living in responsibility, can legitimately make his political decisions too only from that ground of his existence in which he becomes aware of the divine address. When he lets this awareness of the ground be choked off by his group, he is denying God the actual reply.

With "individualism"—the catchword with which groups cover themselves when their inner securities are disturbed by the presence of persons of faith—what I speak of has nothing to do. I hold the individual to be neither the starting point nor the goal of the human world. But I hold the human person to be the irremovable central place of the struggle between the movement of the world away from God and its movement to God. This struggle takes place to an uncannily large extent in the realm of public life; yet the decisive battles of this realm too are fought out in the depths of the person, the ground or abyss.

This generation is striving to escape from the powerfully commanding ever-again of such responsibleness through the flight into a protective once-for-all. The dizziness of freedom of the generation that has just passed has been followed by the search for bondage of the present one, the unfaithfulness of intoxication by the unfaithfulness of hysteria. Only he who knows himself bound to the place where he stands is true to the One Existing and just from that point free for his own responsibility. Not otherwise than out of men who are thus bound and thus free will a form arise that may no longer be called a group but a community. Yet already even now the

---

Fünklein has throughout a more ethical connotation than in Eckhart," which is precisely the case in the Hasidic teaching of the sparks as Buber interprets it—M.F.

man of faith, if he adheres to a cause which is represented in a group, properly belongs to that group; but belonging to it, he must with his whole life, thus also with his group life, remain obedient to the One, who is his Lord. That will at times set his responsible decision against a perhaps tactical one of his group, at times moves him to carry into the group itself the struggle for the truth, the human, the uncertain-certain truth that his deep conscience has drawn forth for him, and thereby to erect in it an inner front or to fortify it. If it is everywhere upright and strong, this front can run as a secret unity across all groups and become as such more important for the future of our world than all fronts that are drawn today between group and group and between associations of groups.

ON THE PROBLEM OF
THE COMMUNITY OF OPINION

For Robert Weltsch

IN A TRULY living community of opinion, the common opinion must ever again be tested and renewed in genuine meetings; the "men who hold the same views" must ever again loosen up one another's views as they threaten to become encrusted, must ever again help one another to confront the changing reality in new, unprejudiced looking. Yes, the reciprocal pointing out, the reciprocal giving-to-see, the reciprocal testing and correcting in the common viewing must be the process through which the opinion is time after time reborn.

Instead of this, one is concerned, in general, with nothing else than holding oneself and the others to what has been laid down; one knows how to suppress in oneself and in the others the strength to reflect from the depths, that is, to draw forth anew the truth-substance of the opinion; the facts are corrected by the light in which one is bound to see them; genuine, hence necessarily tumultouous meetings one successfully avoids; and finally the narrow-minded cliquism, still called community of opinion, is no longer for its adherents any free ground, only a sheepfold. From the state of independence of all which makes possible the living relation of all to all, the human bond has sunk back into the prehuman situation which knows only two essential elements: in the foreground the "this-ness," within which there is no special existence, and breaking forth at times from the background the threatening "that-ness," it too without any personal existence, formless, still only a scheme.

TO THE
CLARIFICATION OF PACIFISM

UNABLE TO take part in your discussions, I shall be with you in spirit with the strength of the wish that you may together recognize a piece of the way that is to be traveled. Taken into the powerfully demanded duty of this place and of this its hour, I can with the written word only contribute a general indication.

The way about which we ask is—insofar as human action is here granted an influence—the way that must be opened up through which the confusion of the present, that appears to us at times like a final chaos, reveals itself in its other essence as the chaos of a new beginning.

Two views concerning the way stand irreconcilably opposed to each other. The one demands that one begin by changing the "relations," for only out of their being different can a change of men and their relationships to one another arise. The other explains that new orderings and institutions in the place of the old will not change one particle of life so long as they are carried by unchanged persons. This alternative is false. One must begin at both ends at once; otherwise nothing can succeed. What new relations really are, even in their operation, depends upon what kind of human existence is put into them; but how shall a new humanity persist on earth if it is not preserved and confirmed by new orderings? The world of man without the soul of it in addition is no human world; but also the soul of man without the world in addition is no human soul. At both ends at once therefore—but that it may avail, a third is needed that cannot be among us without the breath from another sphere: the spirit. The

212

truly new is never an alteration, but an eternal that manifests itself. To me, it is as if two choruses stride about the arena there, the chorus that calls for the orderings and the chorus that calls for the men; their call will not reach its goal until they begin to sing in one: *Veni creator spiritus.*

This can be clarified through the example of war, which is, indeed, more than an example. War will not cease until a genuine representation comprehends and deals with as a whole the territories, raw materials, and the populations of the planet. But this is not enough: men must together become such that they will no longer employ war for any life goal. Both together may lead to the "abolition of war," *i.e.,* to the replacement of war by nonwar. But what is it that we mean when we say that war shall be overcome? A world inventory and world program is still no true understanding of the peoples; men who have renounced all military contests are not yet rid of the other, the elemental war, that ferments between group and group, the silent war between person and person, the secret war in the innermost being of the individuals themselves, all the thousand-named and nameless. The peace of nonwar is not the great peace, the great *Pax,* as it is enthroned in the mural in the *palazzo pùbblico* of Sienna in the midst of the virtues, crowning them all, imperious. What it expresses is no No but the creative Yes of the spirit. That will be lacking if war is only abolished; and then all will be lacking.

The spirit speaks, it speaks an eternal word, a word that can eternally become new because it manifests itself. I will only adduce one of the eternal words of the spirit that in the wording, "Love your neighbor as yourself," has become all too familiar. In truth it says, "Deal lovingly (a dative that is met with only here: what is meant is not a mere feeling but an active attitude of the whole being) with your fellow (*i.e.,* with the man with whom at any time, in any moment you have directly to do), as he who is equal to you (you shall not love him "as yourself" but deal lovingly with him as one who is just as you are, as in need of love, as in need of deeds of love as you). But the Thou that was addressed, when the word was spoken for the first time, was not merely the individual but beyond him also a whole community (Leviticus 19).

It says to man how he should relate to or rather will relate to (for this imperative is really a future, the command conceals a promise) each fellow man that he meets in a living way. But beyond that it says at the same time to the human people how it should relate to each people that it meets in a historical way—or rather how it will relate. This second meaning of the statement has not yet been heard. But even the first, which has again become known in an answer of Jesus, has still barely been heard. We call to the word that it become manifest. *Veni creator spiritus.*

GREETING AND WELCOME

WE OFFER YOU our hearts' greeting of welcome not as the former president of the German Republic, but as Theodor Heuss, the writer of history and the scholar of statehood, the man of living thought and of living word. And nonetheless—this may not remain unmentioned here—when here in the Land your name is named, then one means by that above all the man "who came after Hitler." This does not signify, of course, the notion that in place of Hitler Germany, that meant for us the martyr's death of millions of our people, you had established an "other" Germany. Something of the sort does not take place even in the easiest of cases, and that was certainly the most difficult of its kind in world history. You did not establish at that time the other Germany, but you have represented it now in the renewed freedom of the nation before the nations of the world, as before in the time of self-debasement of the German people and the enslavement of the peoples you had represented it in the persevering and withstanding steadiness of personal existence.

When I spoke to you just now, I almost said: dear fellow colleague; for I think of the fact that we belong together to the collegium of the Peace Prize of the German Book Trade, which I received in 1953 but you received last year, as soon as you were, in fact, no longer the President of the German Bundesrepublik, but again the man Heuss. My eyes still know how at that time, as I stood on the platform, in order to express my thanks to that other Germany that had conferred the prize on me, I saw you sitting before me in the first row, next to my late wife. And my heart still knows how before I began to speak, I first looked at my wife—she who had instilled the lasting presence of a genuine and free Germany into my life. But then I looked at you, in whom was unmistakably manifest to me the German self-faithfulness that had overcome the German self-betrayal. It was obvious to me as symbolic and meaningful that, after the pathos had been soiled and falsified in such a measure, the Germans had set at their head a man of such trustworthy simplicity and a so-deeply-rooted humor. I had already before then understood, certainly, that after the end of that subhuman and antihuman creature that called itself the Führer a humanist must occupy the highest place; but now it became demonstrably clear to me that that could not be the humanist of a program, but only one of self-understood existence.

The antihuman wave that surged up historically with Hitler has its origin in the mistrust of men against one another that has been so strengthened in our time. From this has arisen the reciprocal mistrust of the nations that dominates this world hour. What can prevail against it? When you, honored Herr Heuss, thanked the German Book Trade a few months ago for conferring the Peace Prize on you, you said, "All my life I have been unable to bear the word 'tolerance.'" You have spoken my inmost thought. Nothing is accomplished by men's trying to put up with each other, because nothing merely willed, like this allowing one another to exist, can help; only something that has grown. But what that has grown thus exists? At the conclusion of another address, in which you expressed thanks in the previous year for the conferring of a prize—it was the Hanseatic Goethe Prize*—you spoke, dear Professor Heuss, of the "human trust" that grows in the depths; you called it the presupposition of a democratic form of life. But it is also the presupposition of a genuine

---

* A prize which Buber himself was awarded the year before he received the Peace Prize—M.F.

dialogue that is being opened up between two democracies. We sons of a younger democracy, which knows itself, however, as the heir of ancient promises and biddings, would hearken to your words about the self-formation of democracy as the beginning of such a dialogue.

DIE DREI

In jener so tumultuösen Zeit,
Aus der wir alle widerwillig stammen,
Lebten dreieinig diese drei beisammen:
Freiheit, Gleichheit und Brüderlichkeit.
Doch wenn von drein, die miteinander wohnen,
Zwei kaum was andres sind als Abstraktionen,
Konkretisiert nur durch den Lebenshauch
Der dritten, kann man sich gar leicht entdrein.
Es fliegt sich leicht nach West, nach Osten auch,
Man hat ja hier und man hat dort Verwendung
Für die Ideen—nun nahn sie der Vollendung.

THE THREE

In that so tumultuous time,
From which we all unwillingly stem,
These three lived together, three-in-one:
Freedom, equality, and brotherhood.
Yet if of the three that dwell with one another,
Two are hardly anything but abstractions,
Only concretized through the life breath
Of the third, one can quite easily disband the three.
One flies easily to the West, another to the East,
Yes, one has here and one has there use
For the ideas—now they near completion.

NOVEMBER

Für Ludwig Strauss

Die Rollen brannten langsam und lang.
Ich sah aus der Ferne die Funken stieben,
Ich sah, wie das Pergament zersprang,
Und als ich den Blick zu beharren zwang
Sah ich: die Asche sank.
Nur das Wort ist geblieben.

Die Täter sind nun längst abgetan,
Ein wüster Haufe von Henkern und Dieben.
Mit ihnen ging die Wut und der Wahn
Und die kalte Sucht um den Plünderplan.
Ich sah: geleert die Bahn.
Unser Wort ist geblieben.

Wir aber, sind wir Sprecher dem Wort?
Vermögen zu lauten wirs und zu lieben?
Ich seh uns ringen—um welchen Hort?
Gewaltig der Arm—und das Herz verdorrt?
O Stimme ohne Ort,
Der das Wort ist geblieben!

NOVEMBER

For Ludwig Strauss

The scrolls burned slowly and long.
I saw from the distance the sparks scatter,
I saw how the parchment burst open,
And when I forced my glance to continue,
I saw: the ashes sank.
Only the Word is left.

The destroyers are now long since disposed of,
A vile band of hangmen and thieves.
With them went the rage and the madness
And the cold greed for the plan of plunder.
I saw: the path has become empty.
Our Word has remained.

But we, are we speakers of the word?
Are we able to proclaim it and to love it?
I see us struggling—for the sake of what hoard?
Powerful the arm—and the heart withered?
O homeless Voice
In which the Word remained!

RACHMAN, EIN FERNER GEIST, SPRICHT

Schon kämpfen im krachenden All
Die Götter und die Gespenster,
Da fliegt mir, der Flug ist ein Fall,
Ein graues Vöglein ins Fenster.

Vom Himmel regnen die Gluten,
Blakend birst schon der Erdengrund.
Auf die Bank sehe ichs bluten,
O mein Vöglein, wie bist du wund!

Übers schütternde Weltgewirr
Legt sich ein fahliger Schatten.
Das Auge des Vögleins blickt irr,
Sein Herz ist nah am Ermatten.

Und mag wie Immer er enden,
Der Kampf zwischen Asen und Hel,
Ich hege in zitternden Händen
Das zitternde Israel.

RACHMAN,* A DISTANT SPIRIT, SPEAKS

Already in the cracking All
The gods and the phantoms fight,
There flies to me, the flight is a fall,
A gray little bird into the window.

From heaven the fires rain,
The earth ground bursts already smoldering.
On the bench I see it bleed,
O my little bird, how you are wounded!

Over the shuddering world confusion
A fallow shadow lays itself.
The eye of the little bird glances waveringly,
Its heart is near exhaustion.

And however it ends,
The fight between Ase and Hel,†
I cherish in trembling hands
The trembling Israel.

---

* Rachman may be a play on the Hebrew word *rachmanes,* or
mercy, the merciful attribute of God in the Kabbala—M.F.
† Ase and Hel were kinds of ancient Nordic gods—M.F.

WORLD SPACE VOYAGE

WHAT EFFECT the acquiring of a cosmic mobility will have on man may depend essentially upon how he is in truth constituted today; what strengths and readinesses formerly hidden or misknown will become manifest in the new meetings, what sort of a life substance they will be able to draw forth from these meetings; more exactly, whether the prodigious adventure will awaken a new hybris or a new humility. About that there is nothing that can be determined today because just that in present-day man which is in question here we have not yet succeeded in knowing. I hold it to be probable that occurrences previously existing in the universe will reveal themselves to him more fundamentally than has hitherto happened in the technical age. The current leveling of all surprises will hardly still be practicable.

Man will presumably be forced to prove himself. We shall then learn to know not merely the world but also ourselves anew. What we shall thereby learn about ourselves, that we should today preferably not anticipate.

In all this it is presupposed that the human race united as such will send forth the future satellites and what pertains to them. But that is not yet the case; today they, too, are waves in the general opposition to one another. Whether we overcome this, that is today our concern, on whose progress it depends whether "cosmic" questions in general still have any meaning.

EXPRESSION OF THANKS, 1958

THE OLDER one becomes, so much more grows in one the inclination to thank.

Before all to what is above. Now, indeed, so strongly as could never have been possible before, life is felt as an unearned gift, and especially each hour that is entirely good one receives, like a surprising present, with outstretched thankful hands.

But after that it is necessary time and again to thank one's fellow man, even when he has not done anything especially for one. For what, then? For the fact that when he met me, he had really met me, that he opened his eyes and did not confuse me with anyone else, that he opened his ears and reliably heard what I had to say to him, yes, that he opened what I really addressed, his well-closed heart.

This hour in which I write is an hour of great thanks; *before me* in a beautiful giant box set here by my granddaughter are all the congratulations received on this milestone day of my life-way from men who on the way have met me bodily or spiritually, *and in my memory* all the direct congratulations.

The thanks that I say here to all are not directed to a totality but to each individual.

ZUSEITEN MIR

Zuseiten mir sitzt Melancholie
(So hat einst sie der Meister gesehn).
Sie spricht mich nicht an, sie flüstert nie,
Nur ihres Atems zögerndes Wehn
Trägt zu mir, bis ans innerste Ohr,
Des Geistes Klage, des—wann doch? Wie?—
Das Leben der Seele verlor.

BESIDE ME

Beside me sits melancholy
(Thus once the master had seen her).
She does not speak to me, she never whispers.
Only the hesitant stirring of her breath
Carries to me, unto my innermost ear,
The lament of the spirit which—when then? How?—
Lost the life of the soul.

DER FIEDLER

Für Grete Schaeder

Hier, am Weltrand, habe ich zur Stunde
Wunderlich mein Leben angesiedelt.
Hinter mir im grenzenlosen Runde
Schweigt das All, nur jener Fiedler fiedelt,
Dunkler, schon steh ich mit dir im Bunde,
Willig, aus den Tönen zu erfahren,
Wes ich schuld ward ohne eigne Kunde.
Spüren lass michs, lass sich offenbaren
Dieser heilen Seele jede Wunde,
Die ich heillos schlug und blieb im Schein.
Nicht eher, heilger Spielmann, halte ein!

THE FIDDLER

For Grete Schaeder

Here on the world's edge at this hour I have
Wondrously settled my life.
Behind me in a boundless circle
The All is silent, only that fiddler fiddles.
Dark one, already I stand in covenant with you,
Ready to learn from your tones
Wherein I became guilty without knowing it.
Let me feel, let there be revealed
To this hale soul each wound
That I have incorrigibly inflicted and remained in illusion.
Do not stop, holy player, before then!

EXPRESSION OF THANKS, 1963

AGAIN an hour is come for me in which I have in a special way to render thanks, to thank from far away. That has given me occasion to reflect once again on the verb *to thank*. Yes, it is commonly understood enough, but it does not let itself be easily circumscribed. One notices soon: it belongs to the words that have no associations. In this context I shall cite only two examples.

In German and in English *danken* is connected with *denken, thank* with *think* in the sense of *gedenken*, to *think of*, to *remember* someone: he who says *I thank you* explains to the person he addresses that he will hold him in memory and, to be sure—here that is characteristically self-understood —in a joyous and friendly memory; that one can also keep someone in mind in a very different way is here simply excluded.

It is otherwise in Hebrew. There the verbal form *hodoth* signifies first of all *to avow faith (in someone)*, after that *to thank*. He who thanks avows faith in the one thanked; he wants now and henceforth to avow faith in him. That includes, of course, the *thinking of*, but it is more than that. It does not take place merely within the soul, it goes forth from the soul to the world and becomes action, event in it. But to avow faith in someone means: to confirm him in his existence.

It is my intention to hold in grateful memory and to confirm each person whose good wishes on my eighty-fifth birthday have come to me.

AFTER DEATH

WE KNOW nothing of death, nothing other than the one fact that we shall die—but what is that, dying? We do not know. So it behooves us to accept that it is the end of everything conceivable by us. To wish to extend our conception beyond death, to wish to anticipate in the soul what death alone can reveal to us in existence, seems to me to be a lack of faith clothed as faith. The genuine faith speaks: I know nothing of death, but I know that God is eternity, and I know this, too, that he is my God. Whether what we call time remains to us beyond our death becomes quite unimportant to us next to this knowing, that we are God's—who is not immortal, but eternal. Instead of imagining ourselves living instead of dead, we shall prepare ourselves for a real death which is perhaps the final limit of time but which, if that is the case, is surely the threshold of eternity.

EXPLANATORY COMMENTS

Maurice Friedman

Confession of the Author–1945

Until he was over forty-five, Buber's work as translator and interpreter centered on the legends, stories, myths, and epics of many peoples—Chinese, Japanese, Celtic, Finnish, Jewish, and, of course, Hasidic. Only then did he begin, at first with his friend Franz Rosenzweig, the task which occupied a central place in his life until the time he lost consciousness in his final coma—the translation of the Hebrew Bible into German in such a way as to preserve the original spokenness of the Hebrew.

There is an essential play on words in the German of this poem that it is impossible to reproduce in English. *Schrift* means both any writing and the Scriptures, the Bible. *Schriftsteller* is an author, or writer, one who "places" a *Schrift*, a writing. But in this case the *Schrift*, from being any writing—such as the legends with which Buber was concerned in his earlier years—becomes *the Schrift*, that is the Bible. The other part of the play on words lies in the verb *stellen*, to put or place. From *Schriftsteller*, or author, it develops to the *Schrift*, Bible, which is *erstellt*, achieved, executed, produced.

Ernst Simon, to whom Buber dedicated this poem, was a disciple, friend, and finally colleague of Buber's for forty-five years until the latter's death. Professor of Education at the Hebrew University, Jerusalem, he is Buber's literary executor.

To Create New Words?–1917

From a communication to the International Institute for Philosophy (Amsterdam).

IN HEIDELBERG–1964

Address after the presentation of an honorary doctorate by the University of Heidelberg.

ELIJAH–1903

THE WORD TO ELIJAH–1904

Although these poems emerged in the period when the young Buber was most active in the Jewish Renaissance Movement and in cultural Zionism, the subject of Elijah remained sufficiently central to Buber that it become the theme of his only full-length, mature play, written in 1956 and published in German in 1963.

THE DISCIPLE–1901

From the Cycle "Spirit the Lord."

In a commentary on the German original of *A Believing Humanism,* Buber's old and dear friend Professor Hugo Bergmann, whose relationship with Buber dates almost as far back as this poem, says:

"In the year 1901, the year when, if one may speak thus, Buber 'revealed' himself, as editor of the central Zionist weekly *Die Welt* and then as one of the leaders of the opposition to Herzl at the Fifth Zionist Congress, he wrote for the *Jewish Almanach* a poem that is reprinted here and whose last stanza reads:

> Then the master spoke: "From much wandering
> I took the golden might of the one truth:
> If you can be your own, never be another's."

"It is perhaps not unimportant to note that this truth stems from Paracelsus, the great doctor, thinker, revolutionary of the sixteenth century. ('Alterius non sit, qui suus esse potest.') It was a very proud, I-emphasizing word in the mouth of a young writer unknown outside the Zionist circle." Hugo Bergmann, *"Randbermerkungen zu Buber's 'Nachlese,'" M B (Mitteilungsblatt). Wochenzeitung des Jrgun Olej Merkas Europe,* Tel-Aviv, Vol. XXXIV, No. 22, June 3, 1966, p. 4, my translation.

THE MAGICIANS–1901
From the Cycle "Spirit the Lord."

POWER AND LOVE–1926
Three stanzas for the educational journal *Das werdende Zeitalter*.

THE DEMONIC BOOK–1924
From a *Festschrift* (commemorative volume) for the fiftieth birthday of Anton Kippenberg.

ON THE DAY OF LOOKING BACK–February 8, 1928
Written on his fiftieth birthday, this poem is a compelling witness to the enormous impact on Buber's life and thought of his relationship with his wife Paula. It is dedicated to P. B. (Paula Buber).

DO YOU STILL KNOW IT . . . ?–1949
This poem was inscribed in the copy that Buber gave to his wife Paula of the German edition of *The Tales of the Hasidim*.

SPIRITS AND MEN—1961
The foreword that Buber wrote to the volume containing three earlier books of tales by his late wife.

A REALIST OF THE SPIRIT–1955
To Albert Schweitzer on his eightieth birthday.

MEMORIES OF HAMMARSKJØLD–1962
A talk for the Swedish radio.
In his address at Cambridge University on June 5, 1958, Dag Hammarskjøld devoted one fifth of his talk to a long quotation from "Hope for This Hour," from Martin Buber, *Pointing the Way: Collected Essays,* ed. & trans. by Maurice Friedman (New York: Harper & Bros., 1958), pp. 220-229. "I excuse myself for having quoted at such length from this speech," said Hammarskjøld. "I have done so because out of the depths of his feelings Martin Buber has found expressions which it would be vain for me to try to improve." In my Introduction (pp. vii–viii)

to the 1963 Harper Torchbooks (paperback) edition of *Pointing the Way*, I wrote:

> In a press conference of February 5, 1959, the Secretary-General said, "The moment I get time for it, I would like very much to translate, not the whole volume of *Pointing the Way* . . . but some three or four . . . final essays in the book. . . . I think that he has made a major contribution and I would like to make that more broadly known." In a letter to me of September 25, 1959, Dag Hammarskjøld reaffirmed his intention of translating some of the essays from the "Politics, Community, and Peace" section of *Pointing the Way*, although, he wrote, "again I am in the awkward position of having to give other matters—not all of which are important—professional priority."

ON LEO SHESTOV–1964

Leo, or Lev, Shestov (1866-1938) was a Russian-Jewish religious philosopher and existentialist who had a considerable impact upon European thought in the first decades of this century but is only beginning to be known in America.

ON RICHARD BEER-HOFMANN–1962

Foreword by Buber to Beer-Hofmann, *Gesammelte Werke* (Collected Works).

Richard Beer-Hofmann, an Austrian-Jewish poet, playwright, and novelist, was born in Vienna in 1866 and died, a refugee from Nazism, in New York in 1945. He is best known to English-speaking readers for his book *Jacob's Dream*, translated from the German by Ida Bension Wynn, with an Introduction by Thornton Wilder (New York: Johanesspresse, 1946). His daughters Miriam and Naemah still live in New York and were close to his old friend Martin Buber even in the latter's final years.

HERMANN HESSE'S SERVICE TO THE SPIRIT–1957

Address at the Hesse Celebration in Stuttgart.

Hermann Hesse (1877-1962), the Swiss poet, novelist, and Nobel Prize winner in Literature, is best known to English speaking readers for the very series of novels with which Buber deals in this essay. Hesse and Buber had great friendship and mutual respect, and it was Hesse who nominated Buber for a Nobel Prize in Literature in 1948 as "one of the few wise men living on the earth today."

Hugo Bergmann again supplies us with an illuminating commentary on a passage in this essay:

" 'The spirit has not arisen as a wonderful byproduct of the evolving process of nature; it has appeared to a wonderful natural being, called man, on his way and has entered into him. Paracelsus and following him a poet of our time, Hofmannsthal, know to say of it that it does not dwell in us. I believe, rather, that it does and does not dwell in us.'. . .

"For me this passage offered the greatest difficulties: to what teaching of Paracelsus and Hofmannsthal did Buber refer here? I must thank Werner Kraft . . . for the solution of this literary puzzle. . . .

"Hofmannsthal's poem 'A Dream of Great Magic' contains in its final stanza the three lines:

> Cherub and high lord is our spirit—
> It does not dwell in us, and in the highest stars
> It sets its throne and leaves us greatly orphaned:

These three lines, up to and including the word throne, are a quotation from Paracelsus. Hofmannsthal presumably did not take the quotation from Paracelsus himself, but (this was the helpful hint that was given to me) from Schopenhauer's treatise 'On the Apparent Design in the Destiny of Individuals.' Schopenhauer cites the passages from Paracelsus along with many other passages which state that each individual man has an accompanying genius which presides over his life course. Hence Paracelsus speaks thus: 'In order that the *fatum* be surely recognized, each man has a spirit that dwells outside of him and sets its throne in the highest stars. . . . This spirit is called *fatum*.'

"Paracelsus speaks of the individual man who has his fate; Hofmannsthal seems to want to speak of a spirit of mankind when he says in the poem:

> He felt all men's fate dreamlike,
> Just as he felt his own limbs."*

---

* Hugo Bergmann, *op. cit.*, p. 4, my translation.

AUTHENTIC BILINGUALISM–1963
Foreword to Ludwig Strauss, *Dichtungen und Schriften.*
Ludwig Strauss, whose collected German works this essay introduces, was associated with Martin Buber in Germany and later married his daughter Eva. The two of them preceded Buber to Palestine and lived there together until Ludwig Strauss's death in 1953.

SINCE WE HAVE BEEN A DIALOGUE–1957
Comments on a verse of Hölderlin.
See Buber's comment on Heidegger's interpretation of this passage in Buber, *Eclipse of God, loc. cit.,* "Religion and Modern Thinking," trans. by Maurice Friedman, p. 76.

COMMENTS OF THE IDEA OF COMMUNITY–1951
From a lecture delivered in connection with the "Week of Work at the Comburg" and the discussion concerning it.

COMMUNITY AND ENVIRONMENT–1953
Draft for the Foreword to E. A. Gutkind, *Community and Environment.*

THE THIRD LEG OF THE TABLE–1925

EDUCATING–1960
For the ninetieth birthday of Paul Geheeb, a well-known German educator.

THE TASK–1922

ON CONTACT–1950
From a Jerusalem pedagogical radio talk.

STYLE AND INSTRUCTION–1921
Answer to a circulated question.

AN EXAMPLE: ON THE LANDSCAPES OF LEOPOLD KRAKAUER–1959
The West Manichean Christ figure of Jesus *patabilis* is found in Franz Cumont, Buber stated to Dr. Werner Kraft, and is only preserved in Latin: *"In ligno patet."* Werner Kraft, *Gespräche mit Martin Buber* (Munich: Kösel-Verlag, 1966), pp. 69 ff.

RELIGION AND GOD'S RULE—1923

Leonhard Ragaz was a leading Swiss Christian socialist, closely associated in this cause with Paul Tillich and Martin Buber. On the occasion of his death in 1948 Buber gave a memorial address in Jerusalem. [See Maurice Friedman, *Martin Buber: The Life of Dialogue* (New York: Harper Torchbooks, 1960), p. 279.]

FRAGMENTS ON REVELATION

Written in very different periods of Buber's life.

BELIEVING HUMANISM—1963

Speech of thanks spoken in Amsterdam after the award of the Erasmus Prize.

HASIDUT—1927

After the completion of *Die chassidischen Bücher (the Hasidic Books)*.

Hasidut is a Hebrew word which is most literally translated as piety but which in reality refers to Hasidism, the popular communal mysticism of East European Jewry from the eighteenth to the twentieth centuries whose teachings Martin Buber interpreted and whose legends and tales he retold. The completion of *Die chassidischen Bücher* which is celebrated in this poem marks not an ending but only a middle stage in this lifework of Buber's.

HOUSE OF GOD—1952

Answer to a circulated question about the building for worship of the future.

RELIGIOUS EDUCATION—1930

ON THE SCIENCE OF RELIGION—1928

From a lecture.

PHILOSOPHICAL AND RELIGIOUS WORLD VIEW—1928

Speech made at a session of the Hohenrodter Bund, a group of progressive German educators.

From the end of the First World War through the nineteen twenties Buber was closely associated with the advance movements in German education, represented by the Hohenrodter Bund and the journal *Das werdende Zeitalter,* edited by Elizabeth Rotten and Karl Wilker.

ON THE SITUATION OF PHILOSOPHY—1948

Communication to the Twelfth International Philosophical Congress.

HEALING THROUGH MEETING—1951

Foreword to Hans Trüb's book of the same title.

Hans Trüb was a Swiss psychotherapist who broke away from ten years of doctrinal and personal dependence on Carl Jung under the impact not of Buber's ideas but of his personality. See Maurice Friedman, *Martin Buber: The Life of Dialogue,* pp. 194-197, and the selections from Trüb's writings translated in *The Worlds of Existentialism: A Critical Reader,* edited with Introductions and a Conclusion by Maurice Friedman (New York: Random House, 1964), pp. 497-505.

ON THE PSYCHOLOGIZING OF THE WORLD—1923

Notes for an informal lecture at the Psychological Club of Zurich.

1. Buber is undoubtedly referring here to the school of analytic psychology of Carl G. Jung, a fact of particular interest in the light of the well-known controversy between Buber and Jung over the latter's treatment of religion. (See Martin Buber, *Eclipse of God. Studies in the Relation between Religion and Philosophy* (New York: Harper Torchbooks, 1957), "Religion and Modern Thinking," pp. 78-91, and "Reply to C. G. Jung," p. 137, both trans. by Maurice Friedman.

2. These notes, composed in the same year as the publication of Buber's central work, the poetic little classic *I and Thou,* come as near as anything Buber has written to a more discursive explanation of *I and Thou* (together, of course, with the postscript to *I and Thou* which Buber wrote thirty-five years later for the second edition). By the same token, some central terms in *I and Thou* must be understood in their context there to be understood here. One of these is "the inborn Thou": "In the beginning is relation—as category of being, readiness, grasping form, mould

for the soul; it is the *a priori* of relation, the inborn Thou."
Martin Buber, *I and Thou*, 2nd ed. with a Postscript by the Author Added, trans. by Ronald Gregor Smith (New York: Scrib-
ner's Paperbacks, 1960), p. 27. In *Martin Buber: The Life of
Dialogue* I point out that "the effort to establish relation . . .
comes first and is followed by the actual relation, a saying of
Thou without words. Only later is the relation split apart into
the I and the thing. Hence 'in the beginning is relation,' '*the
inborn Thou*' which is realized by the child in the lived relations
with what meets it. The fact that he can realize what is over
against him as Thou is based on the *a priori* of relation, that is
on the potentiality of relation which exists between him and the
world (p. 60)."

3. This whole passage refers to the next to the last section of
the second part of *I and Thou* (pp. 69 ff.):

—WHAT IS SELF-CONTRADICTION?
—If a man does not represent the *a priori* of relation in his
living with the world, if he does not work out and realize the
inborn *Thou* on what meets it, then it strikes inward. It develops on the unnatural, impossible object of the *I*, that is, it
develops where there is no place at all for it to develop. Thus
confrontation of what is over against him takes place within
himself, and this cannot be relation, or presence, or streaming
interaction, but only self-contradiction. The man may seek to
explain it as a relation, perhaps as a religious relation, in order
to wrench himself from the horror of the inner double-ganger;
but he is bound to discover again and again the deception in
the explanation. Here is the verge of life, flight of an unfulfilled life to the senseless semblance of fulfillment, and its
groping in a maze and losing itself ever more profoundly."

THE UNCONSCIOUS–1957
Notes taken by Maurice Friedman during three seminars at
the Washington (D.C.) School of Psychiatry, March 23rd, March
30th, and April 6th, 1957.

This is the one essay in Buber's philosophical anthropology
that he was unable to write, despite the existence of a notebook
in the Martin Buber Archives of the Jewish National and Uni-

versity Library, Jerusalem, Israel, that shows the most astonishing depth and comprehensiveness of research on the subject. In editing and translating Buber's definitive presentation of his anthropology, *The Knowledge of Man* (New York: Harper and Row and Harper Torchbooks, 1966), I proposed to Buber that he let me include my notes on the three Washington School of Psychiatry seminars devoted to the unconscious as an appendix to this book. He did not want me to do this but preferred instead that I summarize his treatment of the unconscious in Section Eight of my Introductory Essay (Chapter I of *The Knowledge of Man*). I was, therefore, surprised and much moved to learn that Buber's last wish was that my notes should be translated into German and included in *Nachlese*. I have, of course, used my original notes rather than retranslating from the German. My notes on the other sessions—on dreams and psychotherapy—I plan to use in my forthcoming book *Martin Buber: Encounter on the Narrow Ridge* (New York: McGraw-Hill Books, 1968).

Most of the participants in the seminar whose names are mentioned in these notes are or were members of the faculty of The Washington School of Psychiatry and/or of the staff of Chestnut Lodge. One exception was the distinguished Episcopalian theologian, the Reverend Albert Mollegen.

POLITICS BORN OF FAITH

The full significance of this lecture of May 1, 1933, can only be grasped from the fact that it followed a month after the Nazi boycott of the German Jews, the opening gun in Hitler's extermination campaign.

IN TWENTY YEARS–1961

Answer to a circulated question of the press agency Novosti in Moscow.

ON TWO BURCKHARDT SAYINGS–1961

A CONVERSATION WITH TAGORE–1950

Rabindranath Tagore, Indian poet, playwright, and philosopher, was the representative Indian religious figure to generations of Europeans and Americans and still exercises an important impact upon the meeting of India and the West.

CHINA AND US–1928
Speech delivered at the Sessions of the China Institute in Frankfurt am Main.

ON "CIVIL DISOBEDIENCE"–1962
For the hundredth anniversary of the death of Henry Thoreau.

MORE ON "CIVIL DISOBEDIENCE"–1963

ON CAPITAL PUNISHMENT–1928
Answer to a circulated question.

GENUINE DIALOGUE AND THE POSSIBILITIES OF PEACE–1953
Address on the occasion of the awarding to Buber of the Peace Prize of the German Book Trade.

STOP!–1957

ON THE ETHICS OF POLITICAL DECISION–1932

ON THE PROBLEM OF THE COMMUNITY OF OPINION–1951

TO THE CLARIFICATION OF PACIFISM–1939
Message to the training course of the International Peace Academy.

This essay and the four preceding ones might give the reader the impression that Buber was a pacifist. However, he rejected pacifism as he rejected all isms that tempt men to respond in terms of universal timeless principles rather than to the address of the concrete situation. He was rather, as I have called him, "a peacemaker out of the Covenant of Peace." See Maurice Friedman, "The Covenant of Peace. A Jewish Witness" (Wallingford, Pa.: Pendle Hill Pamphlets, 1960 and 1965); Maurice Friedman, *Martin Buber: The Life of Dialogue,* pp. 143-146; and the selections from Buber's "Letter to Gandhi" in *Pointing the Way* and Martin Buber, *Israel and the World* (New York: Schocken Books, 1963).

THE THREE–1960
In an unpublished address by Buber on "Fraternity" to the World Brotherhood Association in California in 1952, Buber

complained that the three principles of the French Revolution—
liberty, equality, and fraternity—have come apart in our day
with the West (the capitalist nations) emphasizing liberty and
the East (the communist nations) emphasizing equality and both
losing sight of fraternity, the social cement which prevents the
other two from becoming empty political catchwords.

NOVEMBER–1948

RACHMAN, A DISTANT SPIRIT, SPEAKS–1942

GREETING AND WELCOME–May 1960
   Address before a lecture by Theodor Heuss in Jerusalem.

WORLD SPACE VOYAGE–1957
   Answer to a circulated question.

EXPRESSION OF THANKS, 1958
   A printed card sent out by Buber in reply to the congratulations sent to him by friends and readers all over the world on
his eightieth birthday.

EXPRESSION OF THANKS, 1963
   A printed card sent out by Buber in reply to messages on his
eighty-fifth birthday.

BESIDE ME–Beginning of 1964

THE FIDDLER–October 1964
   This poem contains two untranslatable puns. One is the contrast between *heilen and heillos* in *heilen Seele* and *ich heillos
schlug. Heilen* carries the meaning of whole, hale, untouched,
innocent, uninjured, intact, even ignorant, whereas *heillos* carries
the double meaning of an incurable wound and of a God-for-
saken, damned, or unholy infliction of that wound. I have used
"incorrigibly" because of its ambiguity, suggesting both an incor-
rigible wound and that the one who inflicts it is himself incor-
rigible in inflicting it. The other pun is in the word *Schein,* which
means illusion, in the sense of being unaware that he inflicted
the wounds but also undoubtedly refers to the contrast that
Buber makes in "Elements of the Interhuman" between the "be-

ing man" who meets others as the person he is and the "seeming man" who tries to appear the way he thinks the other would approve of in order to be confirmed by the other. (See *The Knowledge of Man*, pp. 75-78).

This poem takes on another dimension of meaning if the reader keeps in mind the contrast between being and seeming in Buber's anthropology and its relationship to existential guilt. Because man needs to be made present by others in his uniqueness and to know he is confirmed thus by them in order for his inmost self-becoming to take place, he is tempted to seek false confirmation through trying to appear to them as what he thinks they will approve. The basic temptation of man is to allow seeming to creep into the interhuman and thus destroy the authenticity not only of the interhuman but of the human as such. "To resist this temptation is man's essential courage, to give in to it his essential cowardice." No man is entirely a "being man" and none entirely "seeming," so that all men share to some extent in this injury to the common order of speech-with-meaning that we build up in our relationships with one another. This injury of the common order the foundation of which underlies one's own as well as all other's existence, this guilt taken upon oneself as a person in a personal situation, is existential guilt in the exact sense in which Buber uses it. (See Buber, *The Knowledge of Man*, "Elements of the Interhuman," trans. by Ronald Gregor Smith, and "Guilt and Guilt Feelings," trans. by Maurice Friedman.)

What is so deeply moving about this poem is *not* that Buber composed a poem to illustrate his philosophical anthropology, but that he really lived his philosophy and prayed before death to be given to know and to face his guilt.

Dr. Grete Schaeder, to whom this poem is dedicated, is a German scholar and writer on German literature and philosophy who spent considerable time with Martin Buber between 1961 and 1965 in preparation for her excellent comprehensive study *Martin Buber: Hebräischer Humanismus* (Göttingen: Vandenhoeck and Ruprecht, 1966).

AFTER DEATH—1927
Answer to a circulated question.

BIBLIOGRAPHICAL INDICATIONS

"Reminiscence"—*"Erinnerung."* In *Die Neue Rundschau,* Vol. LXVIII, No. 4, 1957.

"Confession of the Author"—*"Bekenntnis des Schriftstellers."* In *Neue Schweizer Rundschau,* N. F., Vo. XX, No. 3, July, 1952.

"To Create New Words?"—*"Aus einem Schreiben an das 'Internationale Institut für Philosophie.'"* In *Mitteilungen des Internationalen Instituts für Philosophie in Amsterdam,* No. 1, March, 1918.

"In Heidelberg." (Address on the occasion of being awarded the Honorary Doctorate of Philosophy of the University of Heidelberg on November 28, 1964.) Unpublished.

"Elijah"—*"Elijahu."* In *Ost und West,* Vol. IV, No. 12, December, 1904.

"The Word to Elijah"—*"Das Wort an Elijahu."* In *Kadima Kalender für das Jahr 5667.* Berlin: Verlag der Judischen Rundschau, 1906.

"The Disciple" and "The Magicians," poems from the cycle "Spirit the Lord"—*"Der Junger"* und *"Die Magier,"* Gedichte aus dem Zyklus *"Geist der Herr."* In *Jüdischer Almanach.* Berlin: Jüdischer Verlag, 1902.

"Power and Love"—*"Gewalt und Liebe."* In *Das werdende Zeitalter,* Vol. V, No. 1, January, 1926.

"The Demonic Book"—*"Das dämonische Buch."* In *Navigare necesse est. Eine Festgabe für Anton Kippenberg zum 22. Mai 1924.* Leipzig: Spamersche Buchdruckerei, 1924.

"On the Day of Looking Back"—*"Am Tag der Rückschau."* In *Jüdische Rundschau,* Vol. XXXIII, No. 11, February 7, 1928.

"Do You Still Know It . . . ?"—*"Weisst du es noch . . . ?"* Unpublished (1949).

"Spirits and Men"—"*Geister und Menschen.*" (As Foreword) in Georg Munk, *Geister und Menschen.* Munich: Kösel Verlag, 1961.

"A Realist of the Spirit." In Homer A. Jacks, editor, *To Dr. Albert Schweitzer. A Festschrift Commemorating His Eightieth Birthday.* New York: The Profile Press, 1955.

"Memories of Hammarskjøld"—"Erinnerung an Hammarskjøld" (Speech for the Swedish radio, 1962.) Unpublished.

"On Leo Shestov"—"*Über Leo Schestow.*" Unpublished (1964).

"On Richard Beer-Hofmann"—"*Über Richard Beer-Hofmann.*" (As Introduction) in Richard Beer-Hofmann, *Gesammelte Werke* (*Collected Works*). Frankfurt am Main: Fischer Verlag, 1962.

"Hermann Hesse's Service to the Spirit"—"*Herman Hesses Dienst am Geist.*" (Address at the Hesse Celebration in Stuttgart on June 30, 1957.) In *Neue deutsche Hefte,* Vol. XXXVII, No. 8, August, 1957.

"Authentic Bilingualism"—"Authentische Zweisprachigkeit." (As Introduction) in Ludwig Strauss, *Dichtungen und Schriften* (*Poems and Writings*). Munich: Kösel, 1963.

"Since We Have Been A Dialogue"—"*Seit ein Gespräch wir sind.*" In *Hölderlin Jahrbuch 1958–1960.* Tübingen: Mohr (Siebeck).

"Comments on the Idea of Community"—"*Bemerkungen zur Gemeinschaftsidee.*" In *Kommende Gemeinde,* Vol. III, No. 2, July, 1931. In *Neue Wege,* July–August, 1931.

"Community and Environment"—"*Gemeinschaft und Umwelt.*" (Published only in English, as Foreword) in E. A. Gutkind, *Community and Environment. A Discourse on Social Ecology.* London: Watts, 1953. (I have made my own translation of this essay for *A Believing Humanism*—M.F.)

"The Third Leg of the Table"—"*Der dritte Tischfuss.*" In *Selbstwehr,* Vol. XX, No. 13, March 26, 1926. In *Literarische Welt,* Vol. III, No. 51–52, December 22, 1927. In *Die Kreatur,* Vol. III, No. 1.

"Educating"—"*Erziehen.*" In *Erziehung zur Humanität. Paul Geheeb zum 90. Geburtstag.* Heidelberg: Lambert Schneider, 1960.

"The Task"—*"Die Aufgabe."* In *Das werdende Zeitalter,* Vol. I, No. 2, April, 1922.

"On Contact"—*"Uber den Kontakt."* In *Die Idee einer Schule im Spiegel der Zeit. 40 Jahre Odenwaldschule.* Heidelberg: Lambert Schneider, 1950.

"Style and Instruction"—*"Stil und Unterricht."* In Wilhelm Schneider, *Meister des Stils über Sprach- und Stillehre. Beitrage zeitgenössischer Dichter und Schriftsteller zur Erneuerung des Aufsatzunterrichts.* Leipzig: Teubner, 1922.

"An Example: On the Landscapes of Leopold Krakauer"—*"Ein Beispiel. Zu den Landschaften Leopold Krakauers."* In *Merkur,* Vol. XIII, No. 9, September, 1959.

"Religion and God's Rule"—*"Religion und Gottesheerschaft."* In *Frankfurter Zeitung,* April 28, 1923.

"Fragments on Revelation"—*"Fragmente über Offenbarung."* In *Neue Sammlung. Göttinger Blätter für Kultur und Erziehung,* Vol. IV, No. 5, September–October, 1964. In *Für Margarete Susman. Auf gespaltenem Pfad.* Darmstadt: Erato Press, 1964.

"Believing Humanism"—*"Gläubiger Humanismus."* In *Neue Sammlung. Göttinger Blätter für Kultur und Erziehung,* Vol. III, No. 6, November–December, 1963.

"Hasidut"—*"Chassidut."* Unpublished (1927).

"House of God"—*"Haus Gottes. (Stimmen über den Kultbau der Zukunft.)"* In *Eckhart,* Vol. VIII, No. 10, October, 1932.

"Religious Education"—*"Religiöse Erziehung."* In *Das werdende Zeitalter,* Vol. X, No. 1, January, 1931.

"On the Science of Religion"—*"Uber Religionswissenschaft."* In *Jüdischer Almanach auf das Jahr 5689.* Prague, 1929.

"Philosophical and Religious World View"—*"Philosophische und religiöse Weltanschauung."* In *Tagungsberichte des Hohenrodter Bundes.* Vol. II, 1928. Stuttgart, Verlag Silberburg, 1929.

"On the Situation of Philosophy"—*"Zur Situation der Philosophie."* In *Proceedings of the Xth International Congress of Philosophy* (Amsterdam), August 11–18, 1949. Edited by E. W. Beth, H. J. Pos, J. A. P. Pollak. Amsterdam: North-Holland Publishing Co., 1949.

"Healing Through Meeting"—*"Heilung aus der Begegnung."* (As Introduction) in Hans Trüb, *Heilung aus der Begegnung. Eine Auseinandersetzung mit der Psychologie C. G. Jungs.* Edited by Ernst Michel and Arie Sborowitz. Stuttgart: Klett, 1952. ("Healing Through Meeting" was originally published in English in my translation in *Pointing the Way,* Part II—M.F.)

"On the Psychologizing of the World"—*"Von der Verseelung der Welt."* Unpublished draft (1923).

"The Unconscious." Notes taken by Maurice Friedman on a seminar in the Washington (D.C.) School of Psychiatry (1957). (My summary of these three sessions was previously published as Section Eight of my Introductory Essay [Chapter I] to Martin Buber, *The Knowledge of Man,* edited by Maurice Friedman, trans. by Maurice Friedman and Ronald Gregor Smith. New York: Harper Torchbooks, 1966—M.F.)

"Politics Born of Faith"—*"Politik aus dem Glauben."* In *Der Aufbau,* Vol. XXXVIII, No. 41, October 25, 1957.

"In Twenty Years"—*"In zwanzig Jahren."* To the best of Buber's knowledge, his answer to the press agency Novosti, Moscow, was not published (1961).

"On Two Burckhardt Sayings"—*"Zu Zwei Burckhardt-Worten."* In *Dauer und Wandel. Festschrift für Carl J. Burckhardt.* Munich: Callwey, 1961.

"A Conversation with Tagore"—*"Ein Gespräch mit Tagore."* (Only published in English.) In *India and Israel,* Vol. III, No. 4–5, November, 1950. (I have made my own translation of this essay for *A Believing Humanism*—M.F.)

"China and Us"—*"China und wir."* In *Chinesisch-deutscher Almanach für das Jahr Gi Si 1929–30.* Frankfurt am Main: China-Institute, 1929. ("China and Us" was originally published in English in my translation in *Pointing the Way,* Part III—M.F.)

"On 'Civil Disobedience' "—" *'Uber den 'bürgerlichen Ungehorsam.' "* (Only published in English.) In *The Massachusetts Review. A Centenary Gathering for Henry David Thoreau.* 1962. (I have made my own translation of this essay for *A Believing Humanism*—M.F.)

"More on 'Civil Disobedience' "—*"Nochmals über den 'bürgerlichen Ungehorsam.'"* (Only published in English.) In *A Matter of Life.* Edited by Clara Urquhart. London: Jonathan Cape, 1963. (I have made my own translation of this essay for *A Believing Humanism*—M.F.)

"On Capital Punishment"—*"Über die Todesstrafe."* In *Der Mörder und der Staat.* Edited by E. M. Mungenast. Stuttgart: Hädecke, 1928.

"Genuine Dialogue and the Possibilities of Peace"—*"Das echte Gespräch und die Möglichkeiten der Friedens."* Heidelberg, Lambert Schneider, 1953. Frankfurt am Main: Börsenverein deutscher Verleger- und Buchhändlerverbände, 1953. In *Börsenblatt für den deutschen Buchhandel,* Frankfurt Edition, Vol. IX, No. 79, October 2, 1953. In *Neue Schweizer Rundschau,* N.F., Vol. XXI, No. 7, November, 1953. In *Sonnenberg Briefe zur Völkerverständigung,* March 6, 1954. ("Genuine Dialogue and the Possibilities of Peace" was originally published in English in my translation in *Pointing the Way,* Part III—M.F.)

"Stop!"—*"Haltet ein!"* In *Neue Wege,* Vol. II, No. 6, August, 1957. ("Stop!" was first published in English in my translation under the title, "It Is High Time!" in the special "Hydrogen-Cobalt Bomb" issue of *Pulpit Digest,* Vol. XXIV, No. 194, June, 1954—M.F.)

"On the Ethics of Political Decision"—*"Zur Ethik der politischen Entscheidung."* In *Politik und Ethik.* Petzen: Versöhnungsbund, 1933.

"On the Problem of the Community of Opinion"—*"Zum Problem der 'Gesinnungsgemeinschaft.'"* In *Robert Weltsche zum 60. Geburtstag. Ein Glückwunsch, gewidmet von Freunden.* Tel-Aviv/Jerusalem: privately printed, 1951.

"To the Clarification of Pacifism"—*"Zur Klärung des Pazifismus."* (Botschaft an den Schulungskurs der Internationalen Friedens-Akademie, Schloss Greng, 1-12. August 1939.) In *Der Aufbau,* Vol. XX, No. 37, September 15, 1939.

"The Three"—*"Die Drei."* Unpublished (1960).

"November." In *Mitteilungsblatt. Wochenzeitung des Irgun Olej Merkas Europa.* Tel-Aviv, November 5, 1948.

"Rachman, A Distant Spirit, Speaks"—*"Rachman, ein ferner Geist, spricht."* Unpublished (1942).

"Greetings and Welcome"—*"Gruss und Willkomm."* In Theodor Heuss, *Staat und Volk im Werden. Reden in und über Israel.* Munich: Ner-Tamid Verlag, 1960.

"World Space Voyage"—*"Weltraumfahrt."* In *Der Tagesspiegel,* December 25, 1957.

"Expression of Thanks, 1958"—*"Danksagung 1958."* In *Du sollst ein Segen sein.* Edited by E. Horn. Graz, Vienna, Cologne: Verlag Styria, 1964.

"Expression of Thanks, 1963"—*"Danksagung 1963."* Unpublished.

"Beside Me"—*"Zuseiten mir."* Unpublished (1964).

"The Fiddler"—"Der Fiedler." Unpublished (1964). (An unbelievably bad English translation of this poem was published in *The Jerusalem Post* after Buber's death—M.F.)

"After Death"—"Nach dem Tod." In *Münchner Neueste Nachrichten,* February 8, 1928.